Published by Dove and Orca

Copyright, Bobby Newman, Ph.D., 1999

ISBN: 0-9668528-1-8

Second Printing, 2002

Table of Contents

Foreword

Foreword

One day, a family with a child diagnosed with autism called in a behavior analyst to look at their child and provide an evaluation of his current functioning. This is something that happens every day, seemingly nothing out of the ordinary. In this case, however, it *was* out of the ordinary. The family wanted the child looked at before conducting an exorcism because they believed the child to be possessed.

People with autism engage in behavior that can be puzzling to people not familiar with the disorder (and even sometimes to those who are familiar with the disorder). Demonic possession is rarely considered as a theory, however. This warranted a special look.

The behavior analyst was led down into the basement to see the child, Niles. The behavior analyst said "Hi, Niles." Four year old Niles looked the behavior analyst dead in the eye and announced "I am the lone locust of the apocalypse. Think of me when you look to the night sky."

No matter how tough you are, if a four year old tells you that he's the lone locust of the apocalypse and that you should think of him when you look to the night sky, you're going to take a step backwards. In this case, however, after the initial shock wore off, the behavior analyst laughed (leading the family to doubt *his* sanity).

The behavior analyst quickly explained that there was nothing to worry about, that the child was not possessed. He began leading the family through a line of questioning, certain he already knew the answers:

Behavior analyst: "Niles doesn't sleep too well, does he?"

Mom and Dad: "No, he frequently doesn't. Isn't that common for children with autism?"

Behavior analyst: "Absolutely. And I'll bet he likes to watch cartoons, right?"

Mom and Dad: "Yes, that's normal so we encourage it. Is that ok?"

Behavior analyst: "Sure it is. But let me guess, when he can't sleep at night you leave on the cartoon network, right?"

Mom and Dad: "How did you know?" (sounding a bit stunned).

Behavior analyst: "Well, for one thing that's where you find cartoons in the middle of the night. More importantly, I don't sleep too well sometimes and I watch it too. Niles isn't possessed, he's quoting from a television show. On Friday night around midnight they show a program called "Space Ghost: Coast to Coast" on the Cartoon Network. It's a very cool show, based on the David Letterman show. Space Ghost, the cartoon character from the 1970's, interviews real celebrities. His "band leader" is Zorak, the evil mantis. Occasionally the writers forget that he's a mantis and refer to him as a locust. One night he turned to Space Ghost and said "Space Ghost: I am the Lone Locust of the Apocalypse. Think of me when you look to the night sky!" It became a running gag, they've made reference to it in several episodes. I've got them on tape somewhere if you want to see it. This is a common behavior called "echolalia" and we can use it to teach Niles to speak more independently."

What Niles was engaging in was a very common behavior among individuals with autistic-spectrum disorders. It is called echolalia. It takes two general forms. One is immediate echolalia, where the person repeats what you say immediately after you say it. The second type is delayed echolalia, where the person repeats something (s)he has heard hours, days, weeks, or even months ago. This is not a behavior limited to those with autistic-spectrum disorders. One night, driving home from a staff training session in Pennsylvania at about three in the morning, my wife turned to me and said "You know what? I was running this town while you cheap jerks were still eating in diners." It was a line from one of her favorite movies. I replied "Leave the gun...take the canoli" (a line from The Godfather, one of my favorites).

I conceived the idea for this book while giving a mid-term to an experimental psychology class I was teaching at Queens College. I was passing some of the time looking over Irvin Yalom's book, Love's Executioner. This wonderful volume is a collection of stories from Yalom's work as a psychotherapist, and is very enlightening for both professionals and laypersons regarding the nature of the practice of psychotherapy. As I read, it occurred to me that I hadn't seen a similar work intended for parents and professionals who work with people with autism. The muse was upon me. I frantically borrowed a pen and began writing ideas for the book on the back of a spare test paper.

This book is the outcome of that early spark. There is a danger to such a book, however. One very obvious danger is that people will try to use principles that they read about without a fuller understanding of the techniques and principles. This is a risk common to all books that describe or discuss technique. The other danger is a bit more insidious.

When one looks at the section on B. F. Skinner in intro psychology textbooks, one often sees a picture of pigeons playing ping-pong. Students often smile at this and say "how fascinating!" What they miss, however, is that Skinner was not trying to teach pigeons to play ping-pong for its own sake. He was trying to demonstrate the principles of behavior. While I hope the stories contained herein will be interesting, perhaps even entertaining, please don't lose sight of the fact that each chapter was chosen to explore a principle of behavior analysis, an aspect of autism, or a factor in the effective usage of behavior analysis, and not just because "it's a cool story."

Behavior analysis has been growing rapidly over the course of the last few decades. It is has not been without its detractors (see, for example, Newman, 1992, 1996). As Richard Foxx put it at a recent conference, however, "the extent to which people attack behavior analysis is generally an inverse proportion of to what degree they understand it."

Behavior analysis was once considered a crude and simplistic system, a last resort for people with developmental disabilities when all else had failed. Today it stands in the forefront as the treatment of choice for many disorders. This new-found popularity has been a double-edged sword. On the one hand, many more people than ever before are getting the behavior analytic services they need for optimal development. On the other hand, the relative lack of behavior analysts has led to the creation of a whole field of poorly trained "programmers" who apply the principles of behavior analysis with an incomplete (at best) understanding. The results for their students with autism are not always pleasant.

Several states have now begun to certify behavior analysts, as distinct from psychologists, social workers, or other helping professionals. The international Association for Behavior Analysis has taken major steps toward there being a national certification for behavior analysts so that there will be some standard against which claims of expertise in behavior analysis can be measured. We all look forward to the day when behavior analysts can practice as just that, behavior analysts. Sidman (1989) has suggested that behavior analysis has broken away from psychology and is now its own discipline. As someone who has taken both the behavior analysis certification and psychologist licensing examinations, I can attest that the area of overlap between the two disciplines is becoming smaller and smaller. The comparison is like that between chiropractors and osteopaths. They may look at some of the same phenomena, but their methods and background are radically different. A behavior analyst who looks at many of the various treatments offered for autism gets the sickening feeling that (s)he is looking at a medieval magician. My Ph.D. is in psychology, but my field is behavior analysis. It will be a great day when we have departments of behavior analysis at colleges across the country, and the behavior analyst doesn't have to sit, wondering why he or she is there, in a multi-variate statistics course that has nothing to do with her/his discipline.

And by the way, if Niles can be the Lone Locust of the Apocalypse, I henceforth want to be known as the DARK OVERLORD OF BEHAVIOR ANALYSIS. Please refer to Dana Reinecke, my wife and editor and highly skilled behavior analyst, as the DARK MISTRESS OF BEHAVIOR ANALYSIS.

All names in this book have been changed to maintain confidentiality. Where necessary, certain non-essential elements of the narratives have been slightly altered to maintain privacy. Thanks are given to the Association in Manhattan for Autistic Children Inc., its Board of Directors and Professional Advisory Board, and its Executive Director Frederica Blausten for support.

This book is dedicated to Leo and Henrietta Newman, quite possibly the world's most perfect parents.

Chapter One: David Learns to Eat

When David first arrived at the school for children with autistic-spectrum disorders where I am the Director of Training and Resources, he was five years old. He did not and could not eat. All nutrition came exclusively from specially formulated "shakes". David would drink these, but only if they came from the same sippy cup that he was used to.

Early attempts to encourage him to eat had failed. We would hold spoonfuls of food in front of his face, offering other reinforcers if he would take in the food. This is a common form of attempting to ease food refusal. It is based on the PREMACK PRINCIPLE, which states that a high probability behavior can be used as a reinforcer for a low probability behavior. In English, this means that an activity the child likes to engage in (e.g., playing outside) can be used as a reinforcer for a behavior the child does not like to do (e.g., doing math homework). Although the principle seemed sound as far as I was concerned, David was unimpressed. We could not get a bit of solid food into him, despite trying several different types of reinforcers and treatment plans (for example his missing his favorite activities that took place after lunch-time if he hadn't eaten and we were there engaged in the program, like the songs of the day-closing "circle time"). It was months later, and we were still where we had started.

There's an old saying that "you can't shoot pool with rope."

You need the proper tools to do the proper job. If there isn't adequate nutrition going in to support the development of the nervous system, development will be problematic. The shakes might do for David while he was six, but what about when he was 26 or 36? How about the socialization that takes place over food in our culture? It was a problem that needed to be addressed.

We arranged a meeting where David's mother came in to discuss the issue. David's mom expressed concern over the issue as well, and mentioned that she had once tried to eliminate the sippy cup and the shakes. David had simply refused all food for two days rather than alter his eating, more properly his drinking, habits.

David is from an orthodox Jewish family, and it occurred to me that Passover and the highly significant Seder ritual had recently passed. David presumably had sat at the table with the rest of the family taking part in the ritual meal, and he there with his sippy cup. I brought this up and suggested that if we started a bit more of a heavy-handed approach David would be eating everything at the Seder next year. David's mom has always been one to do whatever is necessary to help David and agreed to the plan. One of David's classroom staff asked me if I was really that confident that the plan would work. I replied "It better."

Treatment began the next day. My general plan was to forego the step of David taking food into his mouth voluntarily and to put it in myself. If he spit out the food, I would place it right back in. Reinforcers for accepting food and swallowing would be provided. Only small bits of low consistency foods would be tried at first, with

11

David's shake following the swallowing of just a small bit. David had occasionally accepted some apple sauce or pudding, and these were kept on hand to use as reinforcers as well.

David and I moved to our special spot at the back of the classroom about two hours before he would go home for the day. He had refused the snack offered earlier in the day, so he was without nutrition other than juice since his breakfast shake. I took out a small cracker and held it up to David's mouth. He tried to push the cracker away with his hands and clamp his lips shut. I placed his hands back in his lap and guided the cracker between his lips. I was surprised by the lack of resistance in his lips and jaw, but then realized the muscles were so atrophied that there was little resistance to offer. This also explained why he could not make many sounds. The "bi-labial plosives" (two lipped explosive sounds such as "Puh") can not be formed if the lips lack the strength. His mouth muscles were so atrophied, in fact, that I had to break the cracker with my hand. He was unable to bite down and break it. David began to cry, a sound I would become very familiar with over the next several months. Despite feeling like a big bully who was making this poor child cry, I remembered the image of a family and indeed a whole community seeing their child eat at the Seder for the first time, and contrasted that with an image of the adult David who had never grown up properly due to lack of good nutrition and missed all the socialization opportunities meal times present. We forged ahead.

David sputtered and spit out the bits of cracker. I collected them and placed them back in his mouth. We repeated this ritual several times. It was one we would also become very familiar with. I placed David on my lap to avoid his throwing himself out of the chair and to continue the plan. A few minutes later I became vaguely aware that my lap was warmer than it had been. I had forgotten that David was schedule-trained for the toilet, also not his favorite activity, and I had missed his schedule. David's mom mentioned that she had great difficulty with his toileting at home. I made a mental note that we would have to step up toileting efforts while engaging in the plan, that the new substances in his system would likely cause havoc with his digestion until his body began providing the necessary enzymes to digest the food.

Eventually, the cracker basically dissolved in David's mouth and went down his throat. David took his shake reinforcer (refusing the pudding or apple sauce) and Day One was over. I was wetter, but had seen that it could work. We were all the more determined to see the plan through.

Day Two began with my calling David to bring his chair over to our spot. He did so, with a big smile on his face. I was a bit stunned by this, as I had found the procedure most unpleasant to carry out. I could only imagine how it felt for David, but there he was smiling at me. It was a pattern that we would repeat each day. No matter how rough it ever got, David always smiled and gave me a hug each day whenever we weren't engaged in our struggle. He knows something the rest of us don't.

Day Two went much as Day One had gone, with the exception that I remembered the toileting schedule. I began to co-ordinate this effort more seriously with David's mom. We joked that we were simultaneously dealing with both ends of the digestive tract and one of the staff who was studying developmental psychology made some sort of comment about Freud's Oral and Anal stages of development. I gave her a dirty look, and explained that I would do the jokes.

Over the next two weeks, David began to take in the cracker more easily and without spitting out as much. David even began to pick up the cracker in response to the PROMPT, "David, take food." Confident that we were making progress and that I had a general handle on the procedure, I began to work for generalization. One of the great failures of much programming is to forget that GENERALIZATION does not often occur spontaneously in children with autism, and that it is something you must program for. If I wanted David to eat with people besides myself, he was going to have to practice with others.

I began the generalization effort by having a staff member stand next to me as I did the procedure. After David swallowed his first bit, we changed places such that I was standing and she was sitting and carrying out the procedure. I moved away as they had success, and eventually all staff in the classroom could do the procedure. This is a highly important step that many programs do not focus on adequately. Not only does involving many new people encourage generalization, but more eyes observing can see things that the original trainer might not have seen. The procedure was constantly being refined based on the ideas and observations of the rest of the staff.

The program progressed. The crackers eventually got peanut butter on them for additional texture and nutrition. This was handled well by David, and we decided to make the attempt to include fruit. This worked with some of the "mushier" fruits such as the banana, but did not work for the apple. David would take the small slice of apple into his mouth, but would not swallow. This began to be a problem. David began pooling food in his mouth for long periods of time before swallowing. To attempt to counter this move, I sang with David. His favorite song at that time was the "Five Little Ducks" (you know, the ones who go off one by one until the mommy duck comes looking for them and they have their big family reunion). I would start a verse and stop at the point where Mommy Duck says "Quack quack quack." That was for David to sing, and I wouldn't go on with the song until he quacked. He couldn't do that with a mouth full of food and it encouraged swallowing somewhat. Toileting was pretty consistent at this point.

We continued to press ahead with new foods and began to back off on the shake as he was getting more and more food down. We eliminated the sippy cup. If he was going to have that shake, he was at least going to drink from different cups. We got a chilling blow when mom announced that she had discovered he had slept a whole night with a french fry in his mouth from dinner! His pooling of food and refusing to swallow was getting worse. We were going to have to watch the consistency of the food and make sure to increase it only very gradually. That day, we were not able to get

David to swallow a piece of food and it was time for him to go home. He couldn't ride the bus with food in his mouth anyway due to the choking hazard. I asked David to spit out the food, a futile gesture at best. We had spent so much time working on his not spitting out food when we first started the program that I might just as well have asked him to bench press the bus. I had no choice but to do a finger sweep and remove the food. I did this with a relative lack of concern as I knew of the atrophied condition of his jaw muscles. I was therefore somewhat surprised when David bit down on my finger with enough force to bite through an elephant's hide. My face twisted in pain.

One of the teachers at the school asked me "Problems, Bobby?" She was smiling at me, thinking that I found reaching into David's mouth a bit disconcerting. She didn't realize that I was in real pain. I replied "No, he's biting me." She replied, "I thought he couldn't do that." "HE CAN NOW!"

I eventually had to push in on David's cheeks to free my finger, so forceful was his bite. In truth, small bruises were left on his cheeks from the force I needed to use with my fingers, such was the pressure with which he was biting me. The bite didn't do my finger any good, either.

I got the food out and liberated my finger. I stood there for a moment contemplating my pain and what had just happened. DAVID CAN BITE NOW! I excitedly ran upstairs and called David's mom to warn her about his cheeks and explain what had happened, as well as my new discovery. In typical David's mom

16

fashion, she was concerned about my finger and whether I should go to a doctor and was I OK. To heck with my finger, tomorrow was going to be the first peanut butter sandwich day.

"David, take food." He picked up the sandwich and nibbled off a piece. Staff noted that he would eat into the white part, but avoided the crusts. We're not maniacs, we began to strip the crusts off. David's speed and volume of food consumed increased. Peanut butter gave way to slices of deli meat. That gave way to thin slices of pizza.

I was given an object lesson in personal preferences at this point. The idea of David drinking juice or water with pizza grossed me out, so I asked mom for permission to try to give David soda with the pizza. She agreed that it wasn't the most appetizing sounding combination, pizza and juice. The idea fell flat. David did not like soda and I wasn't going to push it at that point. We're all allowed our personal preferences, although juice and pizza together still gives me the dry heaves.

David came back to the table to eat with the other children as the struggle was gone and he was feeding himself. We needed to stay vigilant and continue to prompt him to eat if he slowed down too much, and he continued to try new foods. Soon, it became apparent that David was no longer refusing new foods in general, just those he didn't like after he tried them. At some point, we all looked at each other and realized that the feeding program was over.

The epilogue of this story came close to Passover of the next year. I had forgotten about the content of our original meeting, but had a tear come to my eye when David's mom left me a phone message that reminded me of my prediction. It had happened. David had eaten everything at the Seder. He had learned to speak over the year, and had even asked for more of some of the food. The whole family and extended neighborhood were ecstatic. Even his dentist was thrilled. The shake had been leaving residue all over his teeth and gums, and the food has scraped it off. Prior to this, David had to be sedated to see the dentist, now he was desensitized to people being around his mouth and he could visit the dentist happily (as happily as any of us, anyway).

As a final note on this story, I want to acknowledge the contribution of all those who were part of the treatment team, their careful observations that helped to move the program ahead, and their dedication. Special note goes to David's mom, who pushed ahead with the tenacity of the proverbial bulldog. She's the type of mom who is a behavior analyst's dream. Not only does she carry through with plans, but she is an open and honest communicator and data collector who writes some of the best notes ever. She is more grateful than she has to be, not taking credit where she should. It's no wonder the staff fight over who gets to sit in her meetings.

When it comes to feeding problems, children with autism show a wide variety of difficulties. There are individual taste issues which sometimes seem to defy explanation. One student would only eat beige food. Another would eat anything, but only if he had french fries with it. No french fries, no other food. I even worked with one student who could detect ONE CC of apple juice in a two liter bottle of cola (I added it in the kitchen, he had no way to know other than smelling it). He could smell the difference if you presented him with three bottles, two pure and one with the one cc of apple juice you added in another room.

Feeding problems can be addressed. The key is perseverance and offering a great deal of reinforcement for the small gains one will initially see. It is also important to determine just what factor the child is "selecting" by (e.g., color, taste, temperature, texture, etc.). A theme that we will return to again and again is that you can help with the behavior problem once you know the function of the behavior. Feeding issues are no different.

Chapter Two: Jim Breaks his Toileting Obsession

I'm enough of an egotist (or enough of a narcissist) that when I get a referral from a figure I truly respect, I still get all excited. Therefore, when I got a phone call in early 1997 from a parent who said they had been referred to me by Richard Foxx, I felt a burst of pride. The family had sought out Dr. Foxx because of his publications and reputation in the area of toilet-training. The Foxx-Azrin toilet-training manual has become a standard in the field, and probably has as wide a circulation as any book in the behavioral literature. The issue the family was dealing with seemed to center around toilet training. The initial conversation went something like this:

"Dr. Newman, we need a toilet training program for our son. We were referred to you by Richard Foxx."

"Call me Bobby. Can you tell me a little about your son?"

"He's 13."

I thought to myself that this was a little older than I was used to dealing with in terms of toilet training, but that makes it all the more important. For a person to be 13 and not toilet trained is all the more significant and therefore all the more important to address. Behavior analysts are generally concerned about behavior that is SOCIALLY SIGNIFICANT, or where the behavior change has real meaning for the person's life. I gathered more information.

"How frequently does your son have urinary accidents?"

"He never has urinary accidents."

"Oh, good. So it's just a matter of bowel training. How frequently does he have bowel accidents?

"He doesn't have bowel accidents."

I thought to myself : he doesn't have urinary accidents, and doesn't have bowel accidents. But he needs toilet training? I asked the next obvious question:

"If he doesn't have accidents, why does he need toilet training?"

"He only goes to the bathroom in a particular way."

(after a pause) "And what way is that?"

"He only moves his bowels on Friday."

"On Friday?"

"On Friday in the afternoon."

"How long has this been happening?"

"Since 1991."

"For the past six years?"

"The doctors said he would grow out of it."

"I hear that a lot."

In truth, I do hear that a great deal. Parents go to medical doctors with legitimate concerns about their children's behavior. They are told that "he'll grow out of it." Four times as many boys as girls are diagnosed with autism. "Boys talk later than girls." "He'll speak when he's ready to speak." "He doesn't need to speak, his sister talks for him." Especially in view of the importance of early intervention (see chapter 20), much greater training in the area

21

of developmental disabilities and developmental disorders must be provided to medical doctors. Every day of delay because "he'll grow out of it" is one day more that the person with autism fails to receive the treatment (s)he needs.

I arrived at the family's home the next Saturday to discuss the case further and what we might do to address his obsessional behavior as regards the toilet. The student, let's call him Jim for the purpose of this discussion, was away from home on a respite outing. I took a walk to his bedroom and noticed that it was extremely neat and tidy. "He probably has some obsessive-compulsive traits," I thought to myself. In retrospect, that was among the more stupid and obvious observations one could make. He moved his bowels only on a given scheduled day during the week, and it didn't occur to me that he might have some obsessive-compulsive behavior until I saw a neat bedroom. It was essential to move ahead with a plan to alter this behavior, as intestinal difficulties had already begun based upon the back-up in Jim' bowels. Medical intervention was imminent.

Not surprisingly, it turned out that Jim had some rituals that he would perform as regards the toilet. He would always have a glass of prune juice in preparation for moving his bowels later in the day. He could read and was interested, again not surprisingly, in the calendar. I therefore went ahead with a rather straight-forward plan based on the assumption that what we were dealing with was obsessive-compulsive behavior, not toilet-training.

I made a new schedule for Jim, and discussed with him what

he would like to earn for learning a new toileting schedule. He decided he would like to stay up late and watch the talk shows. We agreed that Jim would now move his bowels both on Friday AND on Tuesdays. I was teaching psychology at the College of Aeronautics in Astoria at this time, just a short drive over the bridge into Westchester and Jim's home. I explained that I would come to Jim's home on Tuesday evening. If he had moved his bowels by the time I arrived, I would stay just long enough to say "hello." Jim would be able to stay up late to watch a television program he enjoyed. If he hadn't moved his bowels, however, Jim and I would move into the bathroom. We would leave after one of two things happened:

1. Jim moved his bowels
2. The bus came to pick him up on Wednesday morning.

I drove to Jim's home that Tuesday evening, armed with a change of clothes and my toothbrush. As a cardinal rule of behavior management is that you never make a promise you can't or won't keep, I had to be prepared to carry out the treatment plan to its fullest. I can honestly say that I would rather sit through a Spice Girls concert than have spent the evening in the bathroom trying to get Jim to move his bowels. While I would have to classify myself as an agnostic, I found myself talking to the Supreme Being of the Universe on the way over. I promised that I would donate any fees for the evening to charity if Jim had moved his bowels by the time

I got there. The odds of that were slim, considering that Jim hadn't moved his bowels on any day other than a Friday since 1991.

Somewhere in my life, though, I must have actually done something right. When I arrived, Jim's mother met me at the door to announce that Jim had actually moved his bowels that afternoon. Carrying out the treatment plan, I said "hello" and Jim got to stay up late. I called my wife to tell her to cancel the party she was undoubtedly arranging for while I was away. I was on my way home.

Everything thus far had gone according to plan, better than I could have possibly hoped. Progress was not uniform from this point, however. We slowly attempted to add new days to the schedule and indeed to fade out any need for a schedule. I had presumed that once the schedule-dependency was broken that Jim would just begin "listening" to his body's signals and go to the bathroom when he felt like it. Such was not the case. Adding days had to be done slowly, and Jim constantly tested his parents and whether the consequences promised by the evolving treatment would actually be delivered. Jim's parents have had to remain vigilant and keep up on Jim's toileting. Nonetheless, the toilet obsession was broken. Jim did not need continued medical care regarding complications of his bowel habits.

Chapter Three: Alex Learns to Tolerate Separation

An agency where I was directing Parent Training received a phone call from parents who felt at the end of their rope. Alex was a three year old child who was basically making life at home very difficult. He would not, or could not, tolerate anyone being behind closed doors. Any time someone went to the bathroom, or even left the apartment to throw out the garbage, Alex would throw an enormous tantrum. I visited the home and was shown small dents and holes that had been kicked into the bathroom door by Alex.

To meet Alex would never have led one to believe that he was capable of any kind of tantrum. He had a perpetual smile and was very physically affectionate. If you weren't careful, he would hit you with a friendly head-butt that could make your eyes cross or might throw a massive hug on your neck that could cut off your air supply. Alex had a limited, one word vocabulary and speech tended to be used idiosyncratically.

Alex's mother demonstrated the behavior, going into the bathroom. Alex began to cry and then went over and began to bang on the bathroom door. While the tantrum was at its height, mom came out from behind the bathroom door. The treatment plan could be extremely textbook, provided everyone was willing to carry it out.

The BEHAVIORAL CONTINGENCY currently in place was relatively straight-forward. IF you tantrum, THEN mom and dad will come out from behind the door. The reinforcer, mom or dad coming out from behind the door, was coming following the behavior of a major-league tantrum. What we would need to do is to reverse this contingency. Mom and dad would have to come out following calm behavior on Alex's part, not following a tantrum.

To do this would mean carrying out an EXTINCTION procedure. The tantrums would not lead to the reinforcer. Whenever one begins an extinction procedure, however, one must keep in mind a concept known as the EXTINCTION BURST. In everyday language, the extinction burst can be summed up in the phrase, "it's gonna get worse before it gets better." Behavior usually gets worse in one or all of three ways:

1. Behavior bursts in frequency (the person does the behavior more)

2. Behavior bursts in magnitude (the person does the behavior "harder")

3. Behavior bursts in variability (the person does the behavior differently).

You have to plan on the extinction burst when you begin an extinction procedure. Don't begin the extinction procedure if you can not continue the extinction procedure throughout the extinction burst. Otherwise, you run a very serious risk. Consider a person engaging in self-injurious behavior by slapping her head with her hand. You begin an extinction procedure, not reinforcing with attention when she self-abuses. Her behavior bursts. She hits herself more. She hits herself harder. She hits herself in different ways. The open palm becomes closed fist, then it becomes a forearm, then it becomes a forehead slam into the table. What if you can not stand her hitting her head into the table and stop the extinction procedure? Well, what worked in getting her attention was not the head slap, it was the head into the table. When she wants attention in the future, what will she do? Obviously, it is the head to the table. People are quite adaptable. What works is what is done.

What if you *usually* keep to the treatment plan? That can be the kiss of death. To say that you *usually* keep to the treatment plan is to say that you *sometimes don't* keep to the plan and therefore reinforce the behavior. That is called INTERMITTENT reinforcement (as contrasted with CONTINUOUS reinforcement). When reinforcers are given every time the behavior is performed, that is continuous reinforcement. Consider a soda machine. Every time you put your money into the soda machine, you get your soda out. If you don't get your soda out, you have a little extinction burst (kick the machine) and probably won't put more money in. If you do put any more money in, you aren't likely to do it more than once. That's continuous reinforcement, and the extinction burst that follows. With continuous reinforcement, behavior does extinguish relatively quickly after the extinction burst.

Contrast this with intermittent reinforcement. What type of machine do you put money into and often nothing comes out? Obviously, it is a slot machine. Slot machines only pay off every once in a while. What is the behavioral result? People keep on putting money in!!! Behavior maintained by intermittent reinforcement is very long-lasting (resistant to extinction). If you keep to your extinction plan *usually*, you intermittently reinforce the behavior.

Let's bring it back to Alex. To recap, he tantrums when anyone is behind a door. He tantrums until they come out (reinforcer). The reinforcer comes after a variable amount of time of tantrumming (intermittent reinforcement). The procedure, therefore, could not be expected to work very quickly.

This particular extinction procedure we are planning could also be considered a reinforcement procedure. If you stop and think, it's not just an absence of reinforcement for tantrumming, it is a reinforcement procedure. We are reinforcing being otherwise engaged while mom or dad is behind the door. The procedure can roughly be considered a DRO (Differential Reinforcement of Other behavior), also called OMISSION TRAINING or DRZ (Differential Reinforcement of Zero rates). Cool people say "DRO".

To successfully employ a DRO procedure, you identify a particular target behavior that you wish to eliminate. You observe the behavior and determine the conditions under which the behavior generally occurs, including how frequently, how long following the onset of a particular situation, etc. You pick an interval that the person can likely traverse without engaging in the target behavior. You set a timer. If the person goes the entire interval without engaging in the behavior, you deliver the reinforcer. If the person engages in the target behavior before the end of the interval, you reset the timer and say something to the effect of "I'm sorry, you engaged in the target behavior (specify what it is). I need to reset the timer. Let's try again."

I explained these general principles and procedures to Alex's mom and dad, who understood the procedure and even provided their own examples for each of the concepts. We agreed that the tantrums would have to be extinguished. We sketched out a general plan that would include mom or dad going into the bathroom or out into the hallway. They would keep a stop-watch with them and would record how long it took until they got five seconds of quiet from Alex. They would come out from behind the door following the five seconds of quiet. The next day I received a phone call from Alex's mom. She opened by saying "I was in the bathroom for about an hour and ten minutes the first time, is that alright?" Yessssssssss!!! I love when people carry out treatment plans. The behavior, which had been going on for months, was eliminated within two days. Alex's parents were so happy with the progress that they wondered what other gains Applied Behavior Analysis might be able to provide. They began a home program and Alex learned more and more skills. There are times when he'll talk your ear off now, and he beats me at Uno nearly every time we play. He was recently accepted into a class for children with mild language delays in his neighborhood school. He also loves to play tennis and is a big fan of figure skating. I'll play tennis with him, but I draw the line at figure skating. I can only go so far. It's bad enough I had to buy a Bay City Rollers CD for a student who requested it as a reinforcer. The guy behind the counter, who looked like Marilyn Manson complete with white face make-up, said "You still listening to this?" It was all I could do to refrain from asking if he still lived in his mother's basement and thought he was a rock star because he worked in a music store. If I wasn't such a nice guy, there would have been clown-white all over the parking lot.

Chapter Four: Ron Learns to Choose Reinforcers

Once upon a time, a bus driver did not show up to a school where I was conducting an after-school program. The unfortunate fact, I was told by an official of the school, was that I was the only one qualified to drive the bus. I really didn't feel like driving the bus and was obviously not thrilled. My blood ran cold, however, when the woman looked me in the eye and said "I'm sorry, Bobby. I just don't know how to reinforce this moment." My staff looked at me in bewilderment and I shook my head sadly.

The reason my blood ran cold was that this woman was responsible for training all the teaching staff in a public school for children with autism. What she had just demonstrated, however, was a misunderstanding of the most basic concept in behavior analysis or management.

Let's sketch out the basic definition of a REINFORCER. It is anything that follows a particular behavior and increases the probability of that behavior being performed in the future.

(Example: I say "stand up". You stand up. I say "Good standing" and give you a "high five". IF the future probability of your standing up when I say "stand up" increases, then we know that the verbal praise and high five functioned as a reinforcer).

Keeping in mind our definition, a stimulus that increases the future probability of the behavior occurring again in the future, what does it mean to say when you "reinforce a moment?" It means you don't have a clue what you're talking about. While we're on the topic, a good rule to remember is that we reinforce behavior, not people. It is proper to say that we are reinforcing Johnny's *sitting* or Johnny's *talking* or Johnny's *playing*. Don't say you reinforced

Johnny unless you have applied a coat of cement to Johnny's body.

A basic rule to remember is that reinforcers reinforce. If the probability of the behavior does not go up, then you may have delivered a consequence but did not deliver a reinforcer. Consider my favorite example, the one I always use in training: is being tickled a reinforcer? The obvious answer is "it depends." Some people like it, some people don't. The conditions under which the tickle is provided are also very important (by who, how much, when, etc.). My wife likes to listen to Barry Manilow. I'd rather stick needles in my eyes. I love Janis Ian's music, I think it's brilliant. As much as I love her music, she hasn't exactly been tearing up the charts these past few decades.

Reinforcers come in many types. There are the so-called PRIMARY reinforcers. These are reinforcers that we are born with, we do not need to learn to like these. Common examples include food, drink, and some would say physical affection. From the very beginning, though, we see that our definition must be individualized. Would David (chapter one) have found food to be a reinforcer? HE DIDN'T EAT! Obviously, even an M & M (the universal reinforcer) would not have been effective as a reinforcer for David.

The second type of reinforcer is the SECONDARY or CONDITIONED reinforcer. These are reinforcers we have learned to like. Happy face stickers, gold stars, check marks, and some might even say praise, are things we have *learned* to appreciate. We presumably learn to appreciate these reinforcers because they have been paired with more potent primary reinforcers in the past. Now, the commodities have a reinforcing power all their own.

A particularly interesting type of conditioned reinforcer is the GENERALIZED reinforcer. Common examples are poker chips or pennies or stickers or some other type of "token" that gets translated into some sort of "token economy." The token economy is one of the more basic and powerful behavior management tools.

To create a token economy, choose the commodity you are going to use. Pennies or poker chips are common choices. These can be lined with velcro for sticking on a velcro "holding board," or can simply be collected in a cup. This is not an issue in the beginning, as only one token will need to be earned and can be exchanged immediately. Once the commodity has been chosen, begin to "prime" the token. One primes a token by giving the token NONCONTINGENTLY. One then IMMEDIATELY takes the token back and IMMEDIATELY gives a desired commodity. This begins the association process, where the token becomes associated with obtaining the commodity.

After several exchanges of token for commodity, begin doing trials as one would ordinarily. Rather than awarding a primary reinforcer, however, one gives the token (this is the first contingently awarded one) and then takes it back and gives a desired primary. Make sure to use TELEGRAPHIC speech: "Nice talking! You earned a token for such good talking! Here's your token! Give it back and you can have.... (or) What do you want to trade it for?" If (s)he can indicate what (s)he wants to trade for, this can make it more effective.

To begin an intermittent reinforcement system, continue as you had been doing previously. When you award the first token, however, state something to the effect of "Very good playing! Here's a token, put it on your board! When you get one more you can have...Ready for the next one?" The student then needs two tokens to trade in, then three, until one has built up the economy to a level therapists are comfortable with (i.e., keeps motivation high, guards against satiation, and reinforcer consumption is not too time-consuming). Increasing requirements too rapidly can lead to a phenomenon known as "ratio strain." Do not build up too quickly, or you will, in effect, be instituting an extinction procedure.

Now, why should we work to create a token economy system? One of the major reasons is that it is normalizing. What is money, except one big token economy? Money has no value, except what society gives it. "Tickle Me Elmos" and "Cabbage Patch Dolls" were once collectors' items that people were fighting over (I knew a guy who got his nose broken working in a toy store during a cabbage patch doll frenzy). Once it is acknowledged that something has value, people will work for it or spend ridiculous sums for it.

A second reason is that token economies guard against the need for DEPRIVATION and guard against SATIATION. Deprivation means to keep someone without a reinforcer to make it more potent (e.g., not feeding yourself so that you'll be good and hungry when you go to the all-you-can-eat buffet). Satiation means that you've had enough. In other words, you're "full." Primary reinforcers are susceptible to the effects of deprivation and satiation. They only work while you're hungry, and stop working when you're full. Contrast this with a generalized reinforcer. Who do you know who thinks they have enough money? I know only one, my father. He's happy. Everyone else is out pursuing money. Ted Turner owns what, everything? Yet, a few years ago he launched the Cartoon Network. Was it so important that Space Ghost be on in the middle of the night? No, it was presumably an attempt to make MORE money. We don't satiate on a token economy, there's always something new to buy. You're hungry? Buy food! You're thirsty? Buy drink! You're bored? Buy something to entertain you! You're lonely? Buy friends! (well, maybe not that last one, but you get the point).

A last type of reinforcer was mentioned previously, the PREMACK or "activity" reinforcer. This is a favored activity the person earns access to following appropriate behavior. Common examples include play time, access to music or video, entertainment activities and even the controversial "opportunity to engage in perseverative (self-stimulating) behavior".

Ron was a teenage student diagnosed with autism who attended an after-school program where I worked. We were putting together a token economy for Ron to manage his behavior. One of the things I like to do, following the advice of Robert and Lynn Koegel, is to introduce as much choice as humanly possible into the student's day (this decreases tantrums and increases the quality of programs: what better way to choose reinforcers than to ask someone what they want?).

Ron and I assigned commodities to the different numbers of tokens Ron could earn. The most tokens Ron could earn in any particular period was 20. I told Ron "Ok, you can earn a maximum of 20 tokens. To do that, you're really going to have to be on your game. If you get all 20, what do you want to earn?" Ron considered for a moment, then looked me in the eye and said "I want to hang out with Laura" (Laura being one of the staff members).

I must have gotten a little pale as I considered his suggestion. I put Ron on hold and went to speak to my Executive Director. He was something of a religious man and characterized my interaction with Ron as "God calling." I asked for an explanation and he clarified: "Are you a behaviorist or are you a pimp? Are you going to rent staff to the best behaved students?" Before you start to think badly of this situation, Ron was a teenage guy, and if he's interested in spending time with a young woman, that's pretty normalizing to me.

I solved the dilemma in, I think, a reasonable way. I went to ask Laura what she thought of the whole thing. She was flattered that Ron wanted to spend time with her. She agreed they would play basketball together in the gym, with a referee to make sure no one used their hands inappropriately on defense.

Whenever someone comes to me and says that they can't find reinforcers for a particular student, I say "just watch the person." Look at the activities they gravitate towards. You'll find your reinforcers there. Be creative. M & M's are fine, and you use them if they're all you've got, but they're not the most normalizing thing in the world. What do typically developing people "work for?" Can you teach the student to become interested in more normalizing types of reinforcers? I know I'm making progress when my students start telling me that they want to earn money as a reinforcer. Welcome to capitalism.

Chapter Five: George Learns to Exercise

Reinforcers often change across the space of time. Bell bottoms were mercifully gone, and then they came back. Disco was dead, and then some maniac brought it back to life. Fashions come and go. So it is with reinforcers. Something that is reinforcing at one time may lose its power (satiation). Other times, they give way to new reinforcers ("...giant's rings and dragon's wings make way for other toys...").

George was an adult with autism who was terribly out of shape. He was very heavy and could not walk the stairs up to his apartment building without becoming extremely winded. His strength and muscle tone were very low given his weight and he could not lift anywhere near the weight one might expect given his size. Blood pressure was becoming an issue.

George and I attended a YMCA where he enjoyed bouncing around in the pool as I tried to teach him to swim. We would follow this up with a trip out for pizza, and this was how we spent many of our weekends. As it became clear that he was getting more and more out of shape, I began to try to teach George more exercise techniques and to lead him through more and more physical activity (walking on the track, riding the exercise bike, lifting some weights, etc.). I took a personal trainer certification to aid in the effort and to keep it all legal.

To say that George was not happy with the activities would be an understatement. I tried to reinforce George's participation in activities with diet soda and access to preferred activities. This was only partially successful, however, and George let his displeasure be known occasionally with weeping, walking with a pronounced and fake limp, and even feigning throwing up.

I'm sure we made something of a sight at the gym, all 250

pounds of him and all (at that time) 140 pounds of me. We must have looked like something out of an updated production of <u>Of Mice and Men</u>. Our interesting appearance together formed the turning point in the treatment plan. One of the aerobics instructors at the gym came over and asked about what I was doing. I explained that my friend needed to learn to exercise. I introduced her to George, who was spinning on the stationary bicycle. The aerobics instructor (let's call her Kit) approached George and congratulated him on his exercising. I noticed that George kicked it up a notch when Kit came over. The seeds of the new plan were sown.

I enlisted an army of five-foot-nothing bouncy types dressed in leotards as therapy assistants. The entire staff of aerobics instructors would come over and reinforce George's exercising. From that point forward, I could have *lived or died* as far as this behavior program was going. My diet soda or access to reinforcing activities paled in comparison to the praise from Kit and Muffy and Debby and Tammy. I got to sit back in the gym, riding on the bike next to George or leafing through the latest issue of <u>Cigar Aficionado</u>. He and they did all the rest. George, who had resisted going to the gym, now began to request it. In fact, he even perseverated on it a little. That's ok, I did also.

Chapter Six: Bill Learns to Make Appropriate Greetings

As we create programs for children with autism, we sometimes forget some very basic facts. For instance, very few four year olds speak very grammatically or are extremely polite. It is much more common to hear a four year old say "can I?" than "may I?" Those who are concerned with preparing students to join mainstream settings sometimes forget that it may be more important for children to be able to talk about what happened on pro wrestling last night than to know other, more esoteric, information. Knowing how to hang up your coat and get on line may be more important than whether you can describe the difference between things that are living and dead (I'm not kidding, that was the program the kid came in with).

Another falling down point of many programs is that they do not teach for generalization. This is an issue that frequently comes up with parents who are first sending their children to school. The teacher or behavior analyst sends home a program, and the parents look at it and become very angry: "You're out of your mind! My son could do what you have him working on a year ago!! What the heck is wrong with you?!?!?"

Is the programmer truly out of his/her mind? Perhaps not. A failing of many programs is that they do not teach for generalization. The same drills are done each day, in the same order, by the same people, using the exact same instructions, in the same room which is soundproof and has no distractions on the wall. That student then goes into a school where there are other students, where there are distractions on the walls, where staff may change from month to month to encourage generalization, where people may have different accents or be a different nationality than the previous home teachers. The result? The child cannot perform the skill. It's not that he "doesn't know it," but that he has never been trained to generalize. The student may perform at genius levels in his walk-in closet at home with his old familiar home teachers, but shows none of these skills at school. We must remember that if you want generalization, you have to program for it. Generalization does not generally happen on its own.

In order to combat this tendency, a technique called "loose teaching" is employed. Once the student has reached a certain level of mastery of a particular skill, non-essential aspects of the situation are systematically changed. The drills are done in different orders. The drills are done in different rooms. If possible, the drills are done by different people. If all home teachers are female (a common scenario), a male is brought in to work with the child. Hats are worn. Glasses are worn. The phrasing of instructions are varied somewhat. You get the idea.

At one time in my career I was not working with any school, I was only involved in in-home programming. I was traveling all over Long Island, NY, consulting or directing a number of in-home programs for children with autism. One of the students was named Bill.

Bill had achieved great gains during the course of our

programming. While he had once been very resistant to sitting and working, he now sat and worked very willingly. His play skills had improved, and his language was going off the charts. Bill was ready to start school. As I reviewed his programs, however, I realized that a major flaw existed in one of his programs. The "social greetings" program was hopelessly restricted for a child of his age.

We had done a fairly straight-forward social greetings drill. We would say "Hi, Bill" or establish eye contact and wait for him to initiate the greeting. Whoever said "hi" first would then follow up by asking "How are you?" The other would reply and ask how the first person was feeling. The exchange then veered off in any of a number of directions. A major flaw: how many four or five year old children really come up to you and say "Hi, Bobby. How are you? What did you do last night?"

To combat this difficulty, I asked Bill's parents to work on a variety of different greetings over the week until I would see him again. They should practice the types of greeting scenarios he would likely encounter at his new school. I then left the home, and, I'll be honest, I forgot I made this request. I hadn't written it down and had lots of programmatic issues on my mind.

The next week passed, me having forgotten that I had made this request. When I arrived at Bill's home the next week, I absent-mindedly said "Hi, Bill." Bill looked me in the eye and said

"Bob!!! How's your hammer hanging?"

That will bring your memory back in an instant.

"Oh, yeah," I thought to myself. "I did ask them to work on new greetings this week. Somebody took their task VERY seriously.

Bill never had any trouble making or returning greetings at school.

Chapter Seven: Paul Learns
Appropriate Attention-seeking

There is a concept in applied behavior analysis called the RESPONSE CLASS. A response class is all the ways one can execute a behavior that has the same result. Consider all the ways you can turn off a light. You can do it with any finger, or with your elbow, or even with your foot (if you're flexible). If you want to be very sophisticated about it, you can remove the fuse or flip the circuit breaker. All of these responses have the same effect, they turn off the light.

In the world of autism, common responses classes include such things as AVOIDANCE, whereby one engages in behavior that allows one to stay away from situations you don't want to be in. A tantrum is a common avoidance behavior, it allows the individual to get out of unwanted interactions or activities. Another common response class is ATTENTION-SEEKING, any response by the student that gets others to address the student's behavior.

It is a common treatment plan to extinguish inappropriate attention-seeking behavior. As described earlier, however, when you begin an extinction procedure, you have to expect the extinction burst. Before the behavior gets better, it may well get worse. Just how bad can it get? That is sometimes difficult to predict, but we often try to get a sense of the possibilities for the extinction burst during the BASELINE. Baseline is described as that time prior to intervention when we merely observe and collect data on a behavior. After the completion of our baseline we generally introduce our intervention.

The temptation is sometimes to try to by-pass the baseline, and to jump right into trying to eliminate that troubling behavior. This temptation must be resisted, however, for two reasons. First, without that baseline, you will never be truly sure the behavior is improved and that your intervention was responsible. Without making sure to collect data, we might have over or under-estimated how much the behavior was actually occurring. It also might have actually been improving already, and your intervention was not responsible for the noted improvement.

A professor of mine once told me about an individual who had been through a severe automobile accident. He described the individual's behavior and asked me what sort of brain trauma the individual had received in the accident. I gave him my best answer. He then said, "OK, now before the accident this person named his children Omit, Moon Unit, and Dweezil." What I had, of course, forgotten to ask was what the person was like *before* the accident. The person in question was, obviously, the late musician and social critic Frank Zappa. The behavior he initially described that was after the accident was actually no more strange than before the accident. I didn't have the baseline, and botched the call. It's the old joke all over again: "Will I be able to play the piano after the operation?" You can't answer that without knowing if the person could play the piano *before* the operation. Although we may feel certain that we understand a behavior thoroughly prior to intervention, the baseline helps us not only to recognize and maintain behavior change, but to alter our strategies if behavior change is not occurring in the desired direction. It is as important to know if something is not working as it is to know if it is working.

A second reason for the baseline is that it allows you to gather information that will give you a good idea as to the FUNCTION of the behavior. Consider the behavior of "running away." Does the person always look behind them and laugh as people chase and stop running if no one is chasing? That suggests that the function of the behavior is not "running away," but just initiating a game of "chase." If the person always runs to a particular place (like the gym), that is not "running away from somewhere," it's more properly considered "running TO something". The treatment plan will logically be suggested by the function of the behavior. If the person is running because they want to be chased, then make sure the situation is safe and DO NOT CHASE (extinguish the running away).

The third reason for the baseline was alluded to earlier. The baseline allows us to get a sense for how bad an extinction burst is likely to be. One observes the individual and notes all the variations in behavior that they display to see how severe the behavior is likely to become during a full-blown extinction burst.

Paul was a student in a school-age program for children with autism. He was fairly high-functioning, with many academic and social skills. Paul, however, began to display serious attention-seeking behavior soon after transferring to a new class. Paul's attention-seeking behavior included getting up from his seat and dancing or jumping up and down, going to grab toys off the shelf, and putting his hands on other students. The baseline observations suggested that Paul's behavior was indeed attention-seeking.

An attempt was therefore made to extinguish Paul's attention-seeking behavior. His burst began. During an outing to the park, for example, Paul took off his shoe and threw it at an elderly woman on the street before a staff member (who was right next to him) could stop him. Fortunately, Paul missed. I'm not even sure if he was really aiming or just making a show of the act for the attention. In class, when his jumping up and dancing was ignored, he began stripping his clothing off. Staff were sure to reinforce instances of appropriate behavior, but the attention-seeking behavior was slow to extinguish. Situations were complicated by a strange behavioral relationship that soon became evident. For unknown reasons, it was clear that verbal praise, rather than functioning as the reinforcer it was intended to be, was a reliable ANTECEDENT for inappropriate behavior. We were at something of a crossroads. We were not reinforcing inappropriate behavior as called for by the extinction plan, but we were having difficulty due to the fact that our attempts to reinforce appropriate behavior were actually occasioning inappropriate behavior. We considered just delivering a reinforcer (e.g., an edible or toy to play with) without the verbal praise, but this proved ineffective.

46

With this fact in mind, a different scheme for reinforcement of appropriate behavior was instituted and the extinction procedure was modified. We continued to ignore inappropriate behavior on Paul's part. We also, however, instituted a DRO procedure whereby Paul could earn commodities from a menu if a timer went off. The timer, of course, only went off if Paul did not engage in specified attention-seeking behavior for a given interval. If Paul did engage in the behavior, we conspicuously reset the timer immediately upon his beginning the behavior.

A menu of commodities that Paul would choose from was developed, as we thought this would be the means by which we could have Paul experience the most potent reinforcers each time. Presumably, those he selected would be those he truly desired at that moment. The commodities from the menu, it turned out, did not occasion inappropriate behavior the way the reinforcers that the staff had selected, including verbal praise, had.

The system began to work immediately, but had to evolve in keeping with what Paul was "giving us." One humorous incident occurred when Paul's teacher called out to me that Paul had chosen Skittles as a reinforcer and he didn't have any Skittles in the room. I turned into one of the Marx Brothers, sprinting all over the building and bothering everyone in the world for Skittles. I finally found some down by one of the secretaries. I ran back up and gave Paul's teacher the Skittles. I then pointed out that it probably wasn't a great idea to have an item on the menu that wasn't immediately available. Paul's teacher explained that Skittles were not on the menu, Paul had just spontaneously thought of them and patiently waited for them to be produced. Apparently he began to think we could just pull any commodity out of a magic bag. Skittles were then added to the supplies and to the menu for future use. No problems there. Luckily, Paul never asked for anything we could not produce, and following this incident we were sure to limit him only to items that were on the menu and therefore in the room. New items could be added, but he had to choose from the menu. Luckily, Paul accepted this limitation.

One of the interesting things that came out of this system was that Paul would ask for different reinforcers, depending on who was taking care of the timer and reinforcers. A skill I learned somewhere along the line is spinning a basketball on my finger. It doesn't put any points on the board, and I can't shoot worth a damn, but I can look reasonably cool spinning the ball on my finger. One of the teacher assistants came up to me to yell at me about setting up this expectation. Paul had asked him to spin the ball during reinforcer time and he couldn't. We each have our own talents. I can't draw a straight line to save my life.

As time went by, the intervals Paul needed to last without engaging in inappropriate behavior increased in length. During this period, praise also stopped occasioning inappropriate behavior (perhaps because it had been paired with the potent reinforcing commodities from the menu). Today, Paul has no such formal system in place, and merely earns commodities and privileges from the token economy which is in place throughout the entire school.

Those dealing with behavioral issues sometimes make a mistake in that they assume that because a behavior treatment plan is necessary now, that it will always be necessary. In truth, more often it is a case of successfully FADING the treatment plan so that behavioral control is taken on by naturally occurring consequences in the individual's environment. This must often be done gradually. In the case of Paul, for example, the time interval was slowly and gradually lengthened until it matched the token economy already in place in the school. For other students it might entail providing other cues or consequences in the environment to assume behavioral control. This is, however, a crucial step. The requirements of the LEAST RESTRICTIVE MODEL of treatment suggest that we should apply only the least intrusive interventions, while still maintaining our effectiveness. Successfully fading our effective techniques provides us with a means of achieving these twin goals.

Chapter Eight: Jeremy Speaks in School

"Once upon a time there was a young boy who never spoke. Doctors could not find anything wrong, but nonetheless he remained silent. One night at dinner, out of the blue, the child said "Mom, the potatoes are cold." His mother looked at him with a stunned expression and said "You can talk! Why haven't you ever said anything before?" The child replied, "Everything was fine until now."

"A monk joined a monastery where everyone maintained a vow of silence, except for every ten years when they were allowed to say two words. At the end of ten years, he said "Food cold." At the end of twenty years, he said "Bed cold." At the end of thirty years, he said "I quit." The head monk turned and said "I'm not surprised. You've been complaining since you got here."

These two standards of the stand-up comedy world speak to a very serious issue, the generation of speech and the nature of communication. These are crucial issues for students with autistic-spectrum disorders, and sometimes for those with other issues.

One of the more frustrating aspects of autism is the tendency of students to sometimes demonstrate skills in one setting that they do not demonstrate in other settings. We call this a "failure to generalize," and it is a common, if somewhat frustrating, aspect of autism. A child with autism may speak, even fluently, in one situation but not in others. It is all the more frustrating, however, when similar behavior is seen in students who carry no such diagnosis. One such disorder is "elective mutism." Elective mutism is diagnosed when a student will speak in one setting, and not in another. The person might have no other behavioral symptoms and thus would not qualify for a diagnosis of any other disorder, despite this baffling behavior pattern.

We must be careful not to make a very common mistake. The mistake is called engaging in a "tautology." A tautology is a circular definition:

"He's shy!"

"How do you know he's shy?"

"He's standing in the corner, not talking to anyone."

"Why is he doing that?"

"Because he's shy."

"Why doesn't he talk?"

"Because he's mute."

"How do you know he's mute?"

"Well, he doesn't talk!"

As we can see, giving something a label does not mean we understand his behavior or have indeed explained anything. To say that a child is selectively mute is to say (s)he they do not speak in one or more settings, but tells us nothing more about why this is the case.

Jeremy was referred to me by a social worker who had been working with him and his family for nearly a year. Jeremy was a sixth grade student who had never said a word at school, despite the fact that he was capable of speaking fluently. When asked why, he simply said that his teachers were all crazy and he could not provide any other explanation. All attempts to investigate whether any sort of trauma or abuse had occurred led nowhere.

The social worker specialized in bio-feedback and hypnosis. He had been unsuccessful during that year in breaking through the difficulties to get Jeremy to speak at school, using these methodologies. A very bright child, Jeremy scored very high on written reports, but accepted the zeros on oral work. Other children in the school accepted Jeremy, and tried to speak for him. There was apparently one child Jeremy would speak to, but as fate would have it, that child was moving away. Sixth grade would give way to junior high school, and this behavior would become even more unacceptable.

When I first met with Jeremy and his family and his social worker, I was surprised that Jeremy spoke very easily with me. He could not supply any information about why he did not speak at school, just repeating that his teachers and the other students were crazy. Jeremy's parents were extremely frustrated. They had tried, unsuccessfully, to give Jeremy incentives to speak at school. They had offered various reinforcers for speaking, and had even resorted to RESPONSE COST (taking away previously earned reinforcers).

Jeremy expressed a desire to earn the reinforcers, but did not speak. He expressed a desire to avoid the response cost punishment, but still did not speak. Jeremy knew his academic grades would suffer based on his mutism, but still would neither speak nor provide an explanation for the behavior.

The school had assigned a guidance counselor to Jeremy. Jeremy happily spent time with this guidance counselor, listening to him but not replying. Phone consultations with the counselor proved pleasant but uninformative.

I joined in the effort to encourage speaking at school, at first trying a simple contingency contract. Jeremy would be able to choose his own reinforcers for speaking at school, a simple greeting interaction with his favorite counselor. Two weeks of such attempts proved fruitless. Finally, during the third week, a break was hit.

Jeremy was very interested in cards and card tricks. He showed me a trick and then attempted, in vain, to teach me how to do it. I asked him if he had ever shown the guidance counselor that trick or how to do it. He had not. I suggested that we have as our goal for the next school week that he would demonstrate the trick to the counselor. Jeremy said he thought he might be able to do that. True to human form in "waiting until the last minute," it was not until the next Friday that I got a call from Jeremy's counselor. Jeremy had indeed spoken to him, showing him how to do the card trick. He had also said "Good-bye" after their interaction.

I had suspected a form of social phobia to be at the root of Jeremy's refusal to speak. This incident reinforced that theory.

Jeremy was able to speak in this scripted manner, introducing the card trick. If he had to speak spontaneously, there was great anxiety and he "clammed up." Given the structure of the card trick where there was no such social scrutiny, he was in a better position.

Encouraged by this success, we forged ahead. I suggested that next the counselor and Jeremy could play cards. They would play a simple game of Black-jack ("21"). The entire conversation would consist of "hit" or "stick". Jeremy agreed and I called the counselor to tell him that they would be playing this game during their next visit. It was successful.

In an effort to desensitize Jeremy to social interactions beyond the counselor, it was suggested that perhaps a few of his classmates could play, too. Again, there need not be any verbal response beyond "hit" or "stick." This was agreed to by Jeremy, and this occurred several times during the next week. From this point forward, Jeremy began to feel more relaxed. He spontaneously engaged in some discussion during the games, and was gradually able to start speaking at school. He would never win the award for most outgoing, but he was going to be fine.

Several important behavioral processes were at work in this particular case. First, a SYSTEMATIC DESENSITIZATION procedure was in place. Jeremy was moving through a hierarchy of anxiety-provoking situations, only moving on to the next one when he was capable of handling the one before.

Second, we were involved in a SHAPING process. Shaping is technically defined as "the reinforcement of successive approximations to a desired behavior." What this means in English is that we accept a crude approximation at first, but this crude approximation should give way to closer and closer approximations to the desired behavior as time goes on. The general steps to conducting shaping are:

1. Select a target behavior.

2. Assess the best approximation the student can currently perform.

3. Reinforce that approximation.

4. After the approximation is being exhibited reliably, place that approximation on extinction.

5. An extinction burst will set in, which leads to behavioral variability. One of these variations will likely be closer to the target behavior.

6. Reinforce the new, closer approximation.

7. Repeat steps 3-6 until the target behavior is performed.

As we can see, when talking about shaping new responses, the extinction burst can be our friend. Earlier, the extinction burst was seen as a danger for the creation of new and worse behavior problems. While this is indeed true, the extinction burst can also be our friend in that it can help to encourage new adaptive behavior.

Another process which is relevant here is CHAINING. With chaining, one teaches the smaller steps that make up a larger complex multi-step behavior. This can be done either forward or backward, but the principles remain the same.

Lewis Carrol suggested that we should "begin at the beginning, go until we get to the end, and then stop." That is indeed one way of teaching, and we would call it forward chaining. This is not the only way. Sometimes it is also not the most efficient way. There are times when a more efficient strategy is available, and that is what we call "backward" chaining.

To do a backward chaining procedure, one must first break a complex behavior down into the smaller steps that make up the whole "behavior chain." Task analyses generally need to be broken down in terms of complexity for EACH individual student.

When one is doing a backward chaining procedure, one performs every step for the individual, except the last step in the chain. One then prompts the student to perform the last step, and fades that help as possible. Eventually, the student is performing this final step in the chain independently. One can then begin having the student work on both the last step in the chain and the next to last step. Working backwards, one helps the student to become more and more responsible for executing the behavior independently. To take the example of putting on a shirt, you might first put the shirt on the student and perform every step for the student except tucking in the shirt. You might prompt the student through this last step, and fade help as possible. When (s)he is putting on the shirt independently, begin prompting the student to do the next to last step (e.g., poking head through the collar). When they have poked their head through the collar they can perform that portion of the behavior that they have already mastered, tucking the shirt in. Gradually, they become able to perform the entire behavior chain on their own.

Backward chaining can be very effective in that from the beginning, the student sees the finished product ("experiences the terminal reinforcer"). Contrast learning to tie your shoes through backward and forward chaining. With backward chaining, you see the tied shoes from the beginning. With forward chaining, the first step might be "grasp the laces tightly." Why? The terminal reinforcer is very far away, and teaching might not be as effective.

An important caveat to put on this distinction is that some behaviors might not be safe to teach through backward chaining. One would never teach a student to handle sharp utensils without first teaching safety steps. This is where forward chaining comes into play. With forward chaining you do as was suggested, begin at the beginning and teach step by step. Before too long, the entire chain is being emitted.

When there is a behavior that the person is not able to perform, break it down into its requisite steps. Break the step down as far as necessary, beginning where (s)he is, and begin working. A task analysis may be 5 steps or 50. Everything must be individualized, as is a basic tenet of ABA.

Chapter Nine: Evan Learns to Sit at the Table to Work

When one is first beginning discrete-trial teaching with a child with autism, there is frequently avoidance behavior. This will frequently take the form of attempting to leave the setting. One then has the choice of blocking the individual from leaving, possibly having to physically prompt the student back into his/her chair. The other option is to attempt to wait the student out.

The key to this dilemma is, of course, the function of the avoidance behavior. Is the person, for example, seeking attention by running away? Is the problem that your setting is just not enough fun, and the work is all drudgery? These alternate theories suggest different treatment plans.

To begin with, a teaching setting should be as much fun as possible. Give the student as much choice as possible regarding reinforcers and order of tasks to be accomplished. A student is unlikely to want to leave the setting if all the fun stuff is there.

Despite all efforts to make a teaching setting as much fun as possible, there are still students who will try to avoid. One is then left with the choice of trying to block their escape physically, prompting them back after letting them go, or simply letting them go and trying to wait them out or entice them back.

Evan had just begun an ABA in-home program. Things had been progressing well, but Evan had suddenly begun attempting to avoid the teaching setting with all but one of his therapists. He had begun hitting, kicking, scratching, and had even bitten. He would begin sessions by saying "No work!" and would attempt to leave the setting. It seemed that the running away was a simple avoidance response. Preventing the avoidance would cause the attempts to extinguish. This was complicated by the fact that all but one of his therapists were physically unable to contain him there in the setting. A simple extinction procedure would therefore not be possible, and further analysis would prove necessary. Whenever Evan would leave the teaching table, he would run over to the corner and lay down on the ground with his head down. Attempting to get him off the floor escalated the struggle and did not decrease his tendency to avoid.

The only option seemed to be to allow Evan to leave the setting and to not reinforce his struggles with attention. The setting would have to be made as much fun as possible to attempt to eliminate any desire on Evan's part to leave. It was therefore decided that no one would follow Evan or attempt to pick him up. Rather, Evan would be allowed to lay down while the staff would play with favored toys and encourage Evan back to do a little work and play together.

To ensure that the plan was having the desired effect, duration data were collected to measure the frequency and length of Evan's avoidance. As hoped, the frequency and duration of avoidance decreased to zero or near-zero levels over the subsequent weeks, and Evan made rapid progress.

There are many behavioral measures that one can use to ensure the success of treatment plans. Here a few of the most common:

Frequency: This is just a sheer count of the number of times the behavior occurs.

Rate: This is frequency over some unit of time (for example, the behavior occurred five times in an hour).

Duration: How long did the behavior last once it began?

Latency: How long did it take for the behavior to begin once a given stimulus occasioned the response?

Magnitude: This is some measure of the intensity of the behavior (e.g., how hard did he hit, how loud did he scream?).

Percent correct: This is a measure of correct responses out of some total.

Sometimes the function of a given behavior may be obvious, but for whatever reason the logical treatment plan can not be implemented. Perhaps it is not acceptable on ethical grounds. Perhaps the intervention is unacceptable to the child's parents. Perhaps it would be dangerous to implement the procedure (e.g., allowing pica, the eating of non-food substances, to extinguish due to the risk of poisoning). Perhaps it would be dangerous. At an after-school program where I was doing programming, there was a student who was over 300 pounds. He had once hit me sufficiently hard during a tantrum that I suffered a hearing loss. Never in my life did I write an extinction plan for this student, because even if it seemed to be the most appropriate plan, the burst would be too dangerous. His behavior was managed via other plans, and quite successfully.

When managing behavior, there is often more than one option

available. All other things being equal, pick the option that seems most appropriate and follows the Least Restrictive Treatment model. As always, the data guide the decision-making progress. A plan is tried and the data determine its success or failure.

Chapter Ten: Bart Learns to Follow Directions

When Bart first came to the school for children with autism where I was directing programming, he was described as "hyper." This common word was in fact an appropriate description. Bart was out of his seat more frequently than he was in it. Even when we were doing intensive toilet training, Bart was so active that he literally bounced off the wall of the stall of the bathroom at one point. He nearly hurt himself on the toilet paper dispenser, such was his movement without regard for his safety.

Attempts to have Bart sit for discrete trial teaching were frustrated by Bart's inability to sit still. He was large enough that it was difficult to keep him contained in his chair, such was his level of activity. Bart was easily distracted, echolating the verbal imitation trials being engaged in by other students while staff attempted to deliver prompts.

It was becoming clear that Bart was not making the progress we were hoping for. We therefore decided to try something a little different. Bart had begun to follow my directions when I was toilet training him. Another staff member and I took Bart into his own room, and did nothing but work on some basic compliance.

The room we chose was empty, except for one desk, two chairs, and some toys on a low shelf. Bart and I sat to begin discrete trials. We did some easy basic motor and vocal imitation, which Bart excelled at. The reinforcer in use was verbal praise and the opportunity to get up and go play with the toys for two minutes following compliance responses. After a few rounds of success, the staff member and I changed places. She began to work with Bart, following the same basic procedure that I had. In fairly short order, Bart began following directions with this staff member as well.

We then had to generalize back into the classroom. After several hours of Bart receiving reinforcement for compliance and having attempts to leave his seat of his own accord blocked, Bart began to become quite compliant. We accomplished the generalization back to the classroom by bringing Bart back into his classroom when no one was there. His classmates returned one at a time, gradually increasing the levels of distraction and noise.

Progress was not rapid. Bart was still extremely easily distracted by the other students and tested each new staff member that worked with him. Over the course of time, however, Bart progressed sufficiently to move from a class where the greatest emphasis was on one-on-one discrete trial teaching, to one where group instruction was emphasized.

Chapter Eleven: Ernie Takes a Time-out

Time-out is one of those behavior management techniques that has captured the public imagination. It seems that every yuppie household comes equipped with a time-out chair, and I can't remember the last time that I saw a school that didn't have some kind of policy or procedure related to time-out.

Unfortunately, most schools and programs get the technique wrong and do not have the desired behavioral effect. Before we talk about the specifics of time-out, let's go back to our basics of behavior management. Data must be collected on any treatment plan to determine if it is indeed being effective. Too often, treatment plans are continued interminably, without any real consideration as to whether or not they are achieving their desired effect. In the famous "Harry" film, we see an unfortunate individual who exhibits self-abuse for the better part of two decades until a new consultant looks in with fresh eyes and a successful treatment plan is finally designed and executed.

To truly understand time-out, consider the full title: Time-out from positive reinforcement. The idea is to temporarily eliminate, contingent upon inappropriate behavior, positive reinforcement. Typically, the student is taken to another setting away from the positive reinforcement (exclusionary time-out). An obvious implication of this procedure is that the setting to which a person is taken should NOT BE FUN! I observed one school where they showed me their "sad chair." The sad chair was where students were sent when they behaved inappropriately. When I heard about this, I remember thinking that the chair would need a furniture anti-depressant. What the staff at this school did not realize, however, was that it was not a sad chair. In fact, it was a very happy chair. It was happy because students were very happy to sit in it, and that's when chairs are at their happiest. The students were happy to sit in the chair because it was right by the sink, where the students played with the water and toys in the sink while they were in "time out." Students did everything short of having fist-fights over who would get to be in the time-out "sad" chair.

A second obvious implication is that time-out should NOT be used for avoidance behavior. If the student is "acting out" to attempt to get out of the setting, removing him/her is only going to reinforce the behavior and thereby make it MORE likely, not less. This is a basic of functional analysis, but is frequently missed when people employ the "time-out reflex."

Even if time-out is used in keeping with a proper functional analysis, it is sometimes not employed in the most efficient manner possible. Most frequently, time-out is done as "exclusionary," when "inclusionary" time-out can be used. To properly execute a time-out, you merely need to contingently eliminate positive reinforcement. Why not try an "inclusionary" time-out, where the person need not leave the setting and thereby run the risk of accidentally reinforcing avoidance behavior? Often a "time-out ribbon" system is employed. Contingent upon inappropriate behavior, the ribbon takes a time-out and that is a signal to everyone else in the room that the person should not receive reinforcement until their ribbon comes back. This can be just as effective, if not more so, and eliminates the need for a distinct setting that may actually be reinforcing.

One last consideration is the termination of time-out. Too often, time-out ends whenever the timer rings, regardless of what the student is doing. If this is done, one runs the risk of accidentally reinforcing inappropriate behavior by terminating time-out while the person is behaving inappropriately. Time-out should be terminated when the individual is behaving appropriately. If the person is not behaving appropriately when the timer rings, one might say something to the effect of "I'm sorry, you're screaming. I need to set the timer for another minute. Let's try again."

As a final note on the matter, there are formulas in existence for determining how long time-out should be. As a general rule, these formulas are not based on any kind of empirical phenomena. Make it a couple of minutes, no longer is generally necessary (with the proviso regarding the termination of time-out mentioned above).

When Ernie arrived at the school for children with autism, he had a long history of tantrumming to manipulate others. He enjoyed being with the group and engaged in a great deal of inappropriate attention-seeking behavior. A time-out within the classroom was employed when Ernie would begin engaging in inappropriate attention-getting behavior, which often took the form of ear-splitting shrieking.

When placed into time-out, Ernie would attempt to leave. Physically prompting him back to the time-out chair was counter-productive, as Ernie's behavior was reinforced by this interaction. Ernie also sought out attention by calling out to everyone in the classroom by name. The fact that time-out seemed so aversive to Ernie indicated that we were on the right track, but we needed to fine-tune the procedure to ensure effectiveness and eliminate accidentally reinforcing inappropriate behavior.

To make the time-out effective, it was necessary to place Ernie in such a place that he could not escape. This was accomplished by having a staff member sit near Ernie to prevent his leaving the time-out chair. As this attention was likely to reinforce Ernie's inappropriate behavior, the staff member sat with his or her back to Ernie, blocking any escape without speaking or establishing eye contact. To further emphasize that attention was not going to be paid during the time-out, the staff member would sit and conspicuously read a book or pretend to work on a crossword puzzle.

Ernie attempted to defeat the system. He shrieked so as to disrupt class and get reinforcing reactions from the other students. To counter this move, the other students were encouraged to ignore Ernie's calling out. Verbal reinforcement was provided to the other students to encourage the ignoring of the calling out and shrieking. Ernie attempted to engage the person sitting and supervising the time-out. He would speak to him/her, and when no response was forthcoming would attempt aggression such as pulling hair. The staff member would disengage Ernie's hands without addressing the aggression in any other fashion. Ernie then resorted to screaming curses, yelling for the police and echolating phrases about being a bad kid. When all else had failed, Ernie briefly experimented with stripping off his clothing.

When the time-out contingency was first introduced, a five minute time period was used. Ernie was frequently still "out of control" when the timer rang, and would have to "try again" for a period of one minute. As he gained more experience with the system, he learned to sit calmly during the time-out, and soon his behavior outside the time-out setting improved to the point that he rarely experienced time-out in the future. When he did, he announced that he was in time-out and would have to sit nicely. It was actually harder to ignore this statement than the cursing and shrieking, as it seemed more appropriate. It was necessary, however, to prevent encouraging attention-seeking conversation during the time-out.

There are many powerful behavior management techniques to be found within the ABA system. They are only powerful, however, when they are used appropriately and as they were intended to be used. I once visited a school that told me "we tried that behavioral stuff once, it didn't work." ABA is a data-based, self-correcting system. If a behavior management plan is not working, it's either the wrong plan or you're executing it improperly.

Chapter Twelve: Alyssa Plays with Toys

As more and more parents have demanded ABA services for their children, schools and agencies have attempted to respond. When a trained and experienced behavior analyst is not available within the school itself, often a consultant will be called in to try to help with programming and behavior management.

I was asked to provide such consultation at a program offering Early Intervention (EI) services to children with autism. The agency was sincere in its attempt, and not merely providing lip service to the parents. I can't tell you how many programs I have seen that say "We do Lovaas," or "We're an ABA school," and instead of truly dedicating themselves to the system and being trained properly, they offer one half hour of discrete trials to students on a "pull out" model. In effect, they are offering ABA as a related service. ABA is a 24 hour a day philosophy and set of techniques, it is not a related service. Usually, they have xeroxed a few pages out of one of Catherine Maurice's books and proudly say "Look at our programming!"

At this particular agency, they had received some degree of training, and had mastered some basic technique. What was most lacking, however, was any sense of direction and a deeper understanding of exactly why one would work on any particular program. Their motor imitation battery, for example, consisted of over 75 individual, meaningless and arbitrary motions. One child who was brought to my attention was named Alyssa. Her head therapist mentioned something to the effect that "Alyssa had trouble learning the first few imitations, but after that had moved through them pretty quickly." I would hope so.

What was lacking here was an understanding of the concept known as "generalized imitation." When one displays generalized imitation, one has learned the response class of "do what I do," and pretty much any motion that is within the student's physical abilities can and will be imitated. When was generalized imitation mastered, after the first 10? 20? 30? Certainly before the 75th.

To assess for generalized imitation, simply provide "probe" trials. These are trials where you perform a motion the student has never seen before or presumably earned reinforcement for imitating. If the student performs a number of new responses, you can be fairly sure that generalized imitation has been learned.

A central point of any program is "why" we are working on it. In motor imitation, is the goal that the student should learn to clap or touch his nose? No, we have action command (verbs) and body-part identification drills to teach those skills. Obviously, the intent of motor imitation is teach "do what I do." The question remains, to what end? Motor imitation is taught so as to facilitate the learning process. Rather than having to shape each new individual response you would have the person learn, you can simply say "Do this" and demonstrate.

Let us consider "toy play" for a moment. Many children with autism do not spontaneously play appropriately with toys. Motor imitation drills pave the way for appropriate toy play. Why work on

75 arbitrary hand and body motions when you can teach a few basics, teach generalized imitation, and then move into a new program we'd call appropriate toy play. Some of your prompts: "Do this" and roll the car. "Do this" and bang the toy hammer. "Do this" and fly the airplane. "Do this" and color on the page. "Do this" and feed the baby doll. It's a more functional skill than any arbitrary hand or body motion, and is still working on motor imitation if you're concerned that the student still hasn't generalized the skill.

We sometimes forget that there is a deeper purpose behind many of our drills, and they are not being done solely for their own sake. Motor imitation provides such an example. Verbal imitation provides another. We work on individual sounds, but sometimes forget to try to shape those sounds into functional vocalizations as soon as possible. If a student can imitate a one syllable sound, what else can they do? Can (s)he make an "I" sound? That could be the beginnings of a social greetings program ("I" for "hi" and shape from there). Can (s)he make a "sss" or "oh" sound? Why not go for "yes" and "no" drills? Can any of the sounds serve as a label, or as an item they could request? What words or approximations to words can you make from their sounds? Why wait to start working on it?

In Alyssa's case, we moved from motor imitation into toy play. As her parents were very interested in her not developing stereotypes, there were dolls and tools, books and outfits. She learned many play skills, which were eventually turned into activities on an activity schedule so she did not have to be supervised

71

every moment of the day by her parents. She could now sit with a toy and play appropriately. It served her well when she went to kindergarten.

Chapter Thirteen: Jim Stops Biting Himself

When trainees are first learning to work in the applied behavior analytic tradition, they frequently ask how to determine reinforcers for the individuals they are working with. At times, they even lament "I can't find anything he finds reinforcing!"

The first thing to remember if you find yourself in this dilemma is the definition of a reinforcer: a consequence that increases the frequency of the behavior that preceded it. While reinforcers are different across people, and change across time for individuals, there is a relatively easy way to determine reinforcers for each individual.

The "trick" goes back to the Premack Reinforcer concept (a high probability behavior used to reinforce a lower probability behavior). Are there any behaviors that the person engages in at a high rate? You'll find your reinforcers there. The easiest way to think about this is to consider, "what does the individual do if left to his/her own devices?" If (s)he gravitates towards a particular activity, it must be reinforcing.

The ethical and practical dilemma that arises, of course, is that the high probability behavior may not always be socially appropriate. Is it acceptable to have the person earn access to a rolling chair to perseveratively spin? This is an on-going argument in the literature. While of course it would be better if the person could earn socially appropriate behavior as a reinforcer, what if (s)he doesn't have any such behavior at present? You might have no choice but to use access to the socially inappropriate behavior as a reinforcer. The counter-argument claims that this might be confusing to the person: "It's fine for me to perseverate some times and not others? How do I know when?" There's also the issue of "practice makes permanent." The more the person engages in the behavior, the more likely it is to stay in his repertoire. As with most "does the end justify the means" discussions, the issue is settled by answering "some means justify some ends."

This issue came up with Jim, the young man from chapter two with the scheduling obsession. In addition to the toileting issue, he not surprisingly had some other obsessive-compulsive issues. He would insist on doors being completely open or completely closed, for example. He would fix the angle of a pedal on an exercise bicycle and straighten the covers on the bed. In addition to this behavior, Jim engaged in self-biting as an attention-seeking response.

It was difficult to control the behavior, as his parents had difficulty ignoring the behavior (remember, ignore the BEHAVIOR, not the person). Attempts at DRO plans to stop self-biting had been frustrated by our inability to find a powerful reinforcer. Jim was content, it seemed, to sit on the couch, biting himself and rocking.

When we had gone through everything that we thought might be reinforcing, to no avail, a more radical solution was suggested by Jim's mom. Jim's mom and I went around the house, messing it up. As my wife Dana will tell you, that's no trick for me. We opened cabinets half-way. We turned one hanging coffee mug the wrong way. We pulled chairs out from under the table at funny angles. You get the idea.

Our DRO now had a reinforcer. For intervals passed without self-injury, Jim could fix something. Is this treatment plan the highlight of my career, the one I'm most proud of? Certainly not. Especially in view of the rather crude plan for his toileting, I felt like I was being heavy-handed with Jim. Taking advantage of the anxiety he seemed to feel when things were out of place did not exactly make me proud of myself. He had bitten major holes into his forearm, though, which began to resemble a road map. All bets were off. If causing Jim a little anxiety would stop the behavior, and we couldn't find other reinforcers powerful enough, so be it.

As before, the plan worked quickly. We extended the length of time Jim needed to go without self-injury slowly, keeping to the general plan. The DRO helped mom and dad to stick to the treatment plan, and as Jim "got out of the habit" of self-injury, he didn't need to be watched any longer. The behavior simply faded from the repertoire, both at home and at school.

Whenever I left Jim's house, I always felt like something from a Harry Chapin song, exhausted and contemplating the philosophical issues of life. Was this any different from say, a deprivation plan of eliminating soda from a child's life EXCEPT for after toileting successes during an intensive toileting program? Did the ends justify the means? That's for greater minds than mine to ponder. He stopped biting himself. I'll stand behind it.

Chapter Fourteen: Alex Learns to Say "Yes"

You are working with a student who engages in echolalia, the repeating of previously heard words and phrases. This behavior can be very misleading, as you are sometimes unsure if a student is communicating an idea, or merely repeating something heard previously. Even when you have settled the issue of whether or not the utterance is meant to be communicative, it can be very annoying. It also makes students who are echolalic appear different and is thus a prime target for elimination. I love Ray Charles' music, I think he's a musical genius. If I ever meet him I'll be tempted to punch him in the face, blind or not. The reason for this sociopathic behavior? I had to deal with a child who would repeat "You got the right one, uh huh!" fifteen hundred times an hour.

Before completely eliminating the echolalia, remember that you may be able to make use of it. A student who repeats words and phrases can probably be taught to speak functionally more easily than a student who says nothing. Take for example, a student who echolates words and you are attempting to teach him to answer a question. You can say something to the effect of "What's your name, Jimmy." He will repeat "Jimmy." You are now half-way there. The student can answer with the additional prompt of "Jimmy." All you need do now is FADE out that extra help you are providing. This can be done in a number of ways. Perhaps you can say the "Jimmy" softer and softer until you are finally just mouthing the word and then not giving any extra help. Perhaps you can say less and less of the word. "Jimmy" will become "Jim" will become "Ji" will become "Juh" will become nothing. You can also use a "time delay" procedure. Initially you say "what's your name, Jimmy." When you begin your time delay, your prompt will be "What's your name (and then after a 1 second delay) Jimmy". Your next prompt might be "what's your name (and then after a 2 second delay) Jimmy." You continue to add more and more of a delay in between the question ("What's your name?") and the extra prompt ("Jimmy"). In time, students generally begin to answer before you give the prompt, just in response to the question ("What's your name?").

The bottom line with echolalia is that it can be an effective tool. Inappropriate echolalia can be annoying and misleading and make the student appear different. In the initial stages of training, however, it can be used to teach new skills. You might need to make decisions on a program-by-program basis regarding how and when the echolalia will be addressed and eliminated. Don't jump the gun and assume you must eliminate it before exploiting the possibilities echolalia provides.

Let us return to the story of Alex, the young boy who learned to tolerate separation from his parents. Following his rapid success learning to tolerate separation, his parents wondered what else he could learn. As Alex had been heard echolating video programs, it was decided to try to make some of the speech he had more independent and spontaneous. He had only one word that he would use spontaneously, and that was "ok."

Mom expressed a desire that he should be able to say "yes" and "no" rather than "ok." We began to work on this goal. A reinforcer assessment with Alex demonstrated that he liked a great deal of physical play. We therefore decided to make use of this, and parked ourselves on the middle of the living room floor. The first question we would work on was "would you like me to throw you onto the couch?" To take advantage of the echolalia, the question was phrased "Would you like me to throw you on the couch yes."

We began work. The question/prompt were provided to Alex. He excitedly said "ok." The correction was provided, "yes." Alex said nothing. We continued to forge ahead. The question, prompt was repeated. Again, nothing from Alex. Apparently, his echolalia came more easily from the music on the television than from everyday speech. About 45 minutes later, following the question/prompt, Alex looked up and it was one of those times when you can see the wheels turning. He hesitated for a moment and said in a quiet and timid voice "yes." I immediately pitched him onto the couch, where his parents both dove on him like professional wrestlers. He thought this was the funniest thing of all time and within the hour, "yes" became firmly entrenched in his verbal repertoire.

This, of course, was not the end of the program. "Yes" is a distinct response from "no," and there are many different types of questions that call for a "yes" or "no" answer. "Do you want..." (preference) is different from "is this a..." (observation) is different from "is your name..." (factual information). In the beginning, Alex would say "yes" loudly when he meant "yes" and quietly when he meant "no." We needed to correct and shape the verbal responses, and this often comes in gradually. It can sometimes be frustrating when it seems like there's an insight type of experience by the student, and then the skill is not easily demonstrated in the future. Gains are gradual, but they do come.

A funny anecdote related to the development of Alex's language: we were working on a reciprocal conversation drill. This is an interesting drill that teaches the child to speak about themselves rather than just echolating. It might begin with something very simple, such as I'm holding a stuffed Kermit the Frog and he's holding a stuffed Grover (provided he could label both). I would say "I"m holding Kermit." He would have to reply, "I'm holding Grover." In the beginning, most children with autism echolate, but they gradually learn to look at their own situation and reply appropriately. Once a drill such as holding concrete objects is mastered, we can move on to more sophisticated sorts of drills, such as discussing clothing worn ("I'm wearing a blue shirt"), discussing personal information (e.g., "My mommy's name is Henrietta"), and eventually conversation such as exchanging compliments.

Alex was working on a reciprocal conversation drill with his teacher. She probed for vocabulary and conceptual information. "I'm tall," she said. Alex looked at her with a furrowed brow, obviously a bit confused. He sort of looked like a high school student looking at a trigonometry problem he couldn't quite solve. He seemed to have the idea, but lacked the vocabulary. One thing Alex was NOT was tall, he was the shortest student in his class. It occurred to me that he just didn't know the words "short" or "small" or some other word to answer his teacher's comment about her height. She was just about to prompt for the correct answer, when suddenly Alex said "I'm...NOT tall!"

We all laughed. He had gotten us.

Chapter Fifteen: Earl Gets Dressed for School

At parent training meetings, my practice is to present some material for the first one half to two thirds of the period, and to leave the last part for questions about individual behaviors happening at home. In this way, I attempt to show how the techniques and theory we are studying and discussing can be applied to the real-life situations.

One particular evening, an interesting issue was raised. A student had not been in school that day. When I asked why, I was informed that he had refused to go. I inquired for more information and was told that the student had simply refused to go to school. He was not going to get dressed, he wasn't going to eat breakfast, and "he wasn't going to pee."

I didn't miss a beat. "So get him on the bus in his pajamas, and let him hold it in until he gets to school or pees on himself on the bus, and we'll give him breakfast here."

"Are you serious?"

"I'm as serious as a heart attack."

At this point, one of the teachers at the school, who was attending the training to help out, mentioned that "she had once tried to pull the same thing in fourth grade and her mother sent her to school in her pajamas." She never tried it again.

The next day, Earl tried to say that he wasn't going to get dressed or urinate or eat breakfast. Mom told him that he was going to get on the bus hungry, in his pajamas and needing to use the bathroom. Earl replied "But Bobby will be mad when I get to school." Mom shrugged her shoulders. "Your choice." Earl mentioned that his teacher would be mad. "Again, your choice."

Earl urinated, got dressed and ate breakfast. Then he got on the bus. While Earl did test his mom on subsequent occasions, she stuck to her guns and the treatment plan. It stopped being an issue before long.

Bottom line: never overlook the obvious. The truth is, when I suggested the treatment plan, I wasn't thinking of Earl's behavior being affected by my reaction or by that of his teacher. Humiliation is not among my treatment plans. I was thinking in terms of his avoidance behavior not being reinforced by being allowed to miss school again. Still, in this case it wasn't even necessary for the student to experience the consequences of his actions. Sometimes a treatment plan is exactly what you might do with a typically developing child.

Chapter Sixteen: Ellen Stops Perseverating

This chapter is based upon a "Programming Q and A" from <u>The Behavioral Programmer</u> newsletter (a publication of Room to Grow), and is reproduced with permission (Volume 1, issue #3, pp. 1-2). The text from the Q and A went as follows:

QUESTION: We were so happy when my daughter finally learned to say "hello" appropriately. Now, however, she repeats the greeting all day long and it is no longer appropriate. If we do not attend to her "hello," she cries and tantrums. We attend to it sometimes, because we're afraid of the "hello" dropping out entirely, and we worked too hard to get it in the first place. What should we do?

ANSWER: You've got a good few issues tied up in this problem. Fortunately, all can be addressed. Let's start with the easy one first, you're attending to the hello *sometimes*. That's what we call intermittent reinforcement. Intermittent reinforcement leads to behavior that is done for a VERY LONG time, even in the absence of reinforcement. Technically, it is said that intermittent reinforcement leads to behavior that is "very resistant to extinction." Think about a slot machine. It only pays off every once in a while, but people keep dumping in their money. Contrast that with a soda machine (continuous reinforcement). If you don't get your soda, you probably won't put much more money in (little resistance to extinction).

In view of the power of the intermittent reinforcement schedule your daughter's "hello" has been on, it is not likely to extinguish soon. As you point out, we don't want it to. What we DO want, however, is to bring it down to appropriate levels. The way to do that is with a particular type of intermittent reinforcement schedule called DIFFERENTIAL REINFORCEMENT OF LOW RATES of behavior (DRL). With a DRL schedule, you reinforce the behavior IF an acceptable interval has passed since the last response. This gap between responses is called INTER-RESPONSE TIME (IRT).

To implement a DRL schedule, pick an IRT that you think would be appropriate. Base this judgement on how frequently the behavior is being displayed right now. Try to pick an interval that is not too much longer than the current average IRT. Begin attending to responses only if the actual IRT meets or exceeds your goal IRT. If they do not, reset your timer. Gradually increase the IRT requirement, until the response is being emitted at reasonable levels.

As regards the tantrums, you probably the know the answer to that one. They have to be worked through. Give in to a tantrum and you've reinforced it. That means you'll be seeing it for quite a while. Not a very pleasant thought. Tantrums frequently come when a skill (such as waiting) is difficult for a student. If I may quote from one of my favorite old songs, "New born eyes always cry with pain, first look at the morning Sun." The point is that something that is pleasant and beautiful may appear harsh at first. Getting used to it, however, leads one to a lifetime of enjoyment. Learning to accept limits is difficult at first, but it leads to a lifetime of increased opportunity.

At this point, I would be remiss if I did not discuss a basic principle of behavior, NEGATIVE REINFORCEMENT. Negative reinforcement is similar to positive reinforcement in that it is a consequence that *increases* the future probability of a given behavior. It is contrasted with positive reinforcement in that it does so, however, by the WITHDRAWAL of a particular stimulus.

Now, let us consider the frequent course of a tantrum. A request is made of a student. (S)he begins to tantrum. The student may engage in self-injurious behavior, or even aggression towards the person making the request. The temptation is to back off and withdraw the request. This is exactly what must NOT be done, however, as you would be negatively reinforcing the tantrum (withdrawing the request). Rather than truly managing the behavior, you would be encouraging tantrums in the future. Whenever you made a request in the future, the student would go back to what worked before, namely the tantrum.

This is one of the reasons aversives (delivering punishing stimuli) is so dangerous. Punishers are defined like reinforcers. They can be positive (presenting something) or negative (taking something away). In contrast to reinforcers, punishers, by definition, DECREASE the probability of a behavior being emitted again in the future. They are, like reinforcers, individual. Even yelling at or hitting someone might be reinforcing, despite the fact that it seems these might be punishers.

Punishers often work to reduce a behavior. That is what makes them so dangerous. My intentions might be as pure as the driven snow. I see you engaging in dangerous self-injurious behavior. I find this very troubling, and I deliver an aversive. As might be expected, the SIB decreases. Because my greatest desire is to improve your behavior, this is a very reinforcing outcome for me. As nice an outcome as this is, herein lay the danger. The next time the student is engaging in behavior I do not like, I go back and say "Hmm, what worked last time? Oh yeah...." In short order, the most moral person in the world can become a child abuser. This is not a matter of morality, it is a simple behavioral process that is easily predictable with a little knowledge of the laws of behavior.

The slogan of behavior analysts is "Catch 'em being good." Try that first, second, and two thousandth before going to the aversive.

Chapter Seventeen: Greg Stops Vomiting

There are times when a behavior begins for one reason, but then the behavior takes on "a life of its own." This is simply another way of saying that the function of the behavior changes. Take, for example, echolalia. It may at first be a simple language disorder, a common characteristic of autistic-spectrum disorders. Some echolated phrases, however, may get more of a reinforcing reaction than others. The echoed phrase, once neutral to the student and as common as any other echolated phrase, suddenly becomes his most common utterance. "Curse words" often fall into this category. Originally, curse words were merely echoed like any other phrase. Once it is noticed that they get a reaction, however, that may change. At a school where I worked, there was a boy who had learned through this process to put f***ing before words in order to get a reaction from others. Even when asking to see a favored staff member as a reinforcer, he would ask to see "f***ing Jane." (That, of course, became her name for all time: "who's going out? You know, Bob, Linda, F***ing Jane...") It took a great deal of shaping, responding only when he did not use the prefix, to eliminate the word from his vocabulary.

Another instance in which this occurred dealt with Greg, who returned from summer camp with a new avoidance behavior. If he did not want to engage in a particular behavior, he had developed the ability to vomit at will. He returned from camp, vomiting several times a day. This was obviously dangerous, both from a dehydration and electrolyte imbalance issues, not to mention the issue of social inappropriateness.

Information from summer camp was gathered. The story went something like this: one morning, Greg had become sick and vomited following breakfast. Apparently, breakfast did not agree with him. Rather than pushing Greg to partake in activities, which he really didn't enjoy in the first place, he was allowed to simply stay in his bunk for the day. He apparently found being in his bed more reinforcing than the day's scheduled activities. The situation was apparently so reinforcing that he was witnessed making himself vomit the next day. Note what had occurred. Originally he truly had been physically sick. The reaction to his sickness, however, had been so reinforcing that now he was engaging in behavior to try to recreate it. The behavior "had taken on a life of its own."

This was classic avoidance behavior, as witnessed by the fact that the vomiting was exclusively correlated with request avoidance. Because of the physical danger involved in Greg's continuing the behavior, it was necessary to address. I asked Greg to step out with me to go shoot some baskets. He immediately attempted to vomit, and did bring some vomit up. I said something stupid to the effect of "That's very impressive, can we go now?" We left from there, and that was the last of the vomiting I ever saw. The vomiting was successfully extinguished by not allowing Greg to successfully avoid unwanted tasks by vomiting.

There are times when the function of behavior changes, even when it appears to be exactly the same. Another case that is relevant here surrounds Carl, a young boy with autism who suddenly stopped riding the school bus. He would begin yelling "no bus" when his mother attempted to get him ready for school, and he would become physically aggressive. Carl was growing to be too large for his mother to physically prompt him through activity.

Carl had engaged in such behavior previously, in different settings. He would attempt to avoid when he was able to physically intimidate those who were unable to prompt him through activities. I assumed that this was another example of resistance behavior, and went to his home to assist his mother in getting him onto the bus. Carl began to ride the bus again. Following his resumption of bus-riding, however, inconsistencies began to emerge. Carl at one point refused to go back into his home. He began to express concern regarding decorations that had been on the wall for years. It became clear that something else was at work.

What I had assumed was another in a string of avoidance attempts over the years was now seemingly symptomatic of more generalized anxiety issues that would need to be addressed in a different manner. Rather than his not refusing to ride the bus because he knew I would prompt him onto the bus anyway, it seems he was riding the bus because my presence was *comforting*. He knew he would be safe, that someone would have to kill me before anything was allowed to hurt one of my students.

The first moral of the story is that the functions of behavior are not always obvious, even if we think they are. We must constantly reassess, and not believe we have found the answer for all time. As Sherlock Holmes said, "I prefer not to formulate a theory too early. Otherwise one winds up twisting facts to meet theory, rather than theory to meet facts." It is a good motto for us to follow.

The second moral deals with the issue of "dual diagnosis." There was a time when no matter what the student did, we chalked it up to his/her autism. Given that autism is categorized by the American Psychiatric Association as a "pervasive developmental disorder," this made good sense. Autism is *pervasive*, it can affect nearly all areas of functioning. Yet, does this conceptualization possibly leave us missing something? I believe it may.

Take Carl, for example. He seemed to be suffering from an anxiety disorder. How often would we make such a diagnosis in a person with autism? The truth is, we probably wouldn't do it too often. Why should this be the case? Do we believe that autism somehow makes one immune from the development of other disorders? A person with autism may also have seizure disorders, why not anxiety disorders? Why not depression? We sometimes see the development of fetishistic behavior in teens and adults with autism. Is this a result of their autism, or a result of the fact that they are as susceptible to the laws of learning and biology as anyone else is? Probably the latter.

This is an issue on which "the pendulum swings." As we ignored the possibility of dual diagnosis in the past, some doctors are now swinging the other way. The psychiatrist sees the child being extremely quiet, clingy, shy and nervous looking in the unfamiliar setting. (S)he combines that with the eating and sleeping disorders

90

that are frequently seen in both autism and depression, and suddenly EVERYONE leaves their office with a secondary diagnosis of, for example, depression. Prozac or a similar anti-depressant is prescribed, often with little or no benefit.

Should people with autism carry a secondary diagnosis? The answer is, of course, sometimes. We should not just assume that every aberrant behavior we see is due to autism, there may be something else at work. We must also, however, remember all the various areas of functioning autism can affect, and act accordingly.

Chapter Eighteen: Students with Autism Self-manage

Commonly, when I do parent training or consultations with parents, one of their main goals is that their child should be able to be constructively and independently engaged in activities. "I have to watch him 24 hours a day or he'll just sit there stimming" is a common concern. One of the ways that we can attempt to address this concern is by teaching a student self-management skills.

Self-management is one of the most advanced techniques in applied behavior analysis. When a student learns to self-manage, (s)he learns to watch his/her own behavior and deliver reinforcers in keeping with that behavior. It is also one of the most useful skills a student can learn. Students who are able to self-manage require a great deal less trainer time, and are able to function much more easily in everyday environments. As described above, one of the great problems with behavioral teaching for people with autism has always been the failure to generalize. If the trainer is not present, the skill may not be displayed. What if the student WAS the trainer, though? Wouldn't that aid generalization? Of course it would (Cooper, Heron & Heward, 1987; Newman, Buffington, Hemmes & Rosen, 1997).

In this chapter, I will describe a few research studies that colleagues and I have conducted over the last few years. I describe these studies rather than others in the literature only because I was involved in their execution, as with the other case studies described in this volume. Before describing a few studies, though, it would be appropriate to acknowledge the work of Robert and Lynn Koegel, whose earlier work in self-management provided the general framework for the studies we conducted.

One of the difficulties with some behavioral treatments is that they work, but only when others are around to consequate the student's behavior. The student may have learned, for example, that it is inappropriate to flap or rock. When no one is around to address the behavior, however, the student engages in this perseverative behavior. This issue was addressed in the first study I wish to describe, which was published in the journal <u>Behavioral Disorders</u> (Newman, Ryan, Tuntigian, & Reinecke, 1997). In this study, children with autism were taught to self-manage a DRO system to modify their own behavior.

The three students in this study ranged from pre-school through early school-age. All displayed inappropriate perseverative behavior that interfered with the learning process. Two of the students were out of their seats nearly constantly, while a third engaged in self-distracting nail-flicking.

The general framework we have followed for teaching self-management skills can best be described as a fading procedure. Over the course of time, control over consequences is faded from teacher to student, until finally the student is totally responsible for all aspects of the behavior management or teaching program. The three general stages that we conduct are as follows:

1. EXTERNALLY-DELIVERED REINFORCEMENT: This

is a phase that looks very much like a standard behavioral teaching arrangement. The teacher delivers a prompt, the student engages in a particular task, and a given reinforcing consequence is delivered by the teacher.

2. PROMPTED SELF-MANAGEMENT: In this phase, the teacher begins fading control of behavior to the student. Rather than giving a student the reinforcing consequence (e.g., a token on a token economy), the teacher prompts the student to take tokens when (s)he has met criteria for reinforcement. The effort here is to fade, prompting only as necessary until the student becomes independent.

3. SELF-MANAGEMENT: The student judges whether or not (s)he has met criteria and delivers reinforcers with no external prompting.

A common question is whether or not students will "cheat," that is to say take tokens they do not deserve. For the most part, this has not been an issue in the several studies we have conducted over the last several years. In contrast to typically developing students, people with autism tend to "under-reinforce" rather than over-reinforce. They may forget to take tokens they deserve, as opposed to typically developing students who may take more than they deserve. As we will see, this has not hampered the effectiveness of programs, however.

The settings for these interventions were a preschool for children with autism, an in-home program, and an after-school program for children with autism. In this particular study, as in the others, we began by first teaching the students the behavior that would be of concern (out of seat for two students and nail-flicking for the third). This was accomplished through the use of a standard DRO arrangement. An interval was set that the students had to progress without engaging in the behavior that had been targeted for reduction. When they successfully traversed the interval without engaging in the behavior, a timer went off and reinforcers were supplied by staff members.

Following the students' learning of the DRO, we began transferring control to the students. Rather than giving students tokens, we began coaching them to take tokens when they successfully traversed the interval without the target behavior, and prompted when they attempted to take tokens they did not deserve. When the students mastered this skill, we stopped prompting and the students were solely responsible for self-reinforcement. Their behavior did not suffer, despite the fact that the students were not as reliable in delivering reinforcement as the staff member conducting the intervention had been.

We were gratified that students were able to maintain their behavioral gains when assessed at follow-up. Rather than the students requiring a staff member to watch over their behavior and deliver consequences, they became able to observe and modify their own behavior.

This was an example of self-management being applied to reduce an inappropriate behavior. Other studies aimed at the creation of more appropriate behavior. In Newman, Buffington,

O'Grady, McDonald, Poulson and Hemmes (1995), we used a similar procedure to teach teenage students to follow a schedule and to identify the time for transitions. All were perfectly capable of engaging in appropriate activities, but were what we would call "prompt-dependent." They waited for directions from staff before engaging in tasks, and often engaged in those tasks until told to stop regardless of whether the task was accomplished. The students learned to follow a schedule, and therefore became much more independent and self-reliant. They did not need to be watched and supervised, which was our goal.

Other studies examined similar self-help behavior that served to make the students more independent and socially appropriate. Reinecke, Newman and Meinberg (in press) taught students with autism to share their favorite toys with other students. Newman, Buffington and Hemmes (1996) taught teenagers with autism to engage in more advanced conversation.

What must be remembered is that self-management is a behavior like any other. It consists of two responses, self-monitoring (watching oneself) and self-reinforcement (delivering consequences for one's own behavior). These are responses that can be taught, and must sometimes be monitored by outside agents. Self-management IS behavior, and must be treated like any other behavior.

Chapter Nineteen: The Do's and Don'ts
of Speaking about ABA

"The white-jacketed doctors are evil, and as extreme
version of B. F. Skinner's behaviorists...
understandably so" (Petix, 1987, p. 94)

"If one were seeking an illustration to place above a
Skinnerian caption, such as 'The Inclination to
Behave' or 'Operant conditioning' or 'Beyond
Freedom and Dignity,' one could hardly find one
more vivid and arresting than the picture of Malcolm
McDowell in the role of Alex licking the
sole of the actor/antagonist's shoe"
(Aggeler, 1979, p. 175).

These quotes were taken from literary critics who were
commenting on Anthony Burgess' novel, <u>A Clockwork Orange</u>.
While their discourse can simply be dismissed as that of people
unfamiliar with the true nature of ABA, it is unfortunately a rather
widely held view of the field. It therefore must be addressed.

The popular stereotype of the behavior analyst is that of the
cold intellectual who is interested only in controlling others.
Frequently an atheist, (s)he holds no greater philosophy than the
manipulation of behavior without regard for the rights and wrongs

of any particular applications, or indeed any greater philosophy. As explained to me when I was an undergraduate, (s)he is someone no one at the school wants to talk to or associate with. Everyone else would prefer that the behavior analyst would just stay in his or her coffin, until a student is throwing the furniture through the window. When all else has failed, reluctantly, someone knocks on the coffin and the behavior analyst rises up like Dracula to supply a behavior treatment plan. Having served his or her purpose, the behavior analyst returns to his or her coffin until called upon again.

Late in my undergraduate career, I decided that I would like to branch out a bit beyond the psychology I was studying. Having become interested in humanist philosophy during high school, I decided to take the training that would allow me to become an Ethical Culture leader, sort of a non-theistic minister. The training would take two years of part-time study, and would begin with a weekend seminar at the Ethical Culture Society in New York City. The session began with everyone going around the circle and saying their names and telling what they did for a living. There were various Unitarian ministers, counselors, social workers, and all sorts of people who did all sorts of nice things. When it got to me, I, in my best matter-of-fact tone, announced that I was a student of behavior modification. From the stiffened reactions, you would have thought that I said I throw babies into furnaces. I remember thinking: "Now I know how Peter, Paul and Mary must have felt singing 'Blowing in the wind' at West Point."

Now, I'll admit that I did make this pronouncement for some

shock value. I've always been sensitive about the bad image of ABA and wanted to be very "in your face" about it, given that I was going to be studying with these people for the next two years. I've since learned to tone it down a bit, and have successfully discussed ABA with a wide variety of groups over the last decade or so. I'd like to share some of the "do's and don'ts" these experiences have taught me. Obviously I will have to be speaking in stereotypes, quite antithetically to the individualized nature of ABA. Please use these only as alterable guidelines and not as commandments carved in stone. Judge your audience and behave accordingly.

"ABA Parents"

Before speaking about how to discuss ABA in a diplomatic and effective fashion with the unconvinced, I would like to touch on a group that demands no quarter, and gives none. These are people who need no convincing. I am speaking of the "ABA parent," a unique and impressive variety. These are frequently the parents of children with autism who have come to study and desire ABA for their children, often inspired by the writings of Catherine Maurice. Of all the groups I will discuss, these people tend to want to see and hear something that vaguely resembles the stereotype of the behavior analyst that others find objectionable (without the vampire overtones, of course).

These parents are the hard-core supporters and advocates of ABA. They want a behavior analyst who is an expert. They want someone who is no-nonsense. Although you can be a character personally, treatment must be all business and empirically-based.

They want someone who is demanding of the child, helping him or her to reach all reasonable goals. These parents are looking for behavior analysis to be applied in an efficient manner to help their children to make their maximum progress. These parents tend to have little patience for unproven treatments or incompetent practitioners, and expect the same in their ABA therapists. In fact, to appear weak on the unproven treatment is to risk losing their faith. You can say "I don't know," but generally on the way to "and this is how we figure it out." You'll run into these parents at the conferences, and they read the literature. They respect the cuts and bruises your body may have taken over the years, they have them too. You earn their respect and they carry through on your plans. They tend to be political activists, lobbying for effective treatment and expect you to do the same. These parents have often invested enormous financial resources in obtaining services for their children, right down to mortgaging the house.

Do's and don'ts: DO cite your background and credentials. As ABA has become more popular, many parents have become wary and cynical of those who are poorly trained and merely trying to "cash in" where demand outstrips supply. DO come "dressed to work." If it's a day to demonstrate technique with children, too nice an outfit indicates that you're not "hands on." DO cite the literature, many of the parents will either be familiar with it already or want to look it up. DO discuss the limitations of the field, but also discuss new areas of research that might address these deficits. DO use technical jargon as well as everyday language. Many of the parents will use jargon as well. DO feel free to discuss previous cases, successes and failures. These parents are anxious to engage in discussions of what worked and why, as well as what didn't and why. DO mention extreme cases and know that these parents may be able to tolerate more graphic examples, including video-tapes, of inappropriate behavior than the uninitiated. These parents pride themselves on being realists. DO discuss the basic principles of behavior and the history of behavior analysis as well as the applications. These parents are anxious to know everything they can about the techniques and the field. DO require that parents begin taking data on behavior immediately so that they can start addressing their concerns. DO give homework on Day 1. DO emphasize "more advanced" concepts such as generalization. DO provide programs that will be done both at home and at school or other applied settings.

DON'T appear too soft on unproven or ineffective treatments. DON'T just be an armchair expert. Talk from personal experience. DON'T engage in discussions that disparage other ABA practitioners. There seems to be some unwarranted rivalry between some schools or proponents of particular teaching methodologies that is just not helpful to the field or to the parents. Frankly, everyone is tired of it. DON'T be ignorant of the educational and political bureaucracies the parents face in trying to obtain ABA services for their children.

Dana and I were doing an observation of a student at a school one morning. We were pointed in the general direction of the student and, to my shock, found him completely enclosed and hanging inside a burlap sack being swung back and forth in a doorway. This was all being done in the name of a sensory integrative therapy. Dana, who is the nice one, quickly said "Don't make a face." I couldn't stop myself. I share this story, as well as my shock and disgust, with the ABA parents. When discussing this incident with our next group, a bit more tact is called for.

Non-ABA (or "soon to be ABA") Parents

The non-ABA parent of the child with autism is different than the ABA parent. They are frequently just learning about their child's condition, and may not yet have come to grips with it. In a lecture that has stuck with me over the years, Claire Poulson once warned a graduate ABA class that behavior analysts should never expect to ever be the most popular kids on the street. Because ABA doesn't promise a quick miracle cure, but only years of hard work, it may never be the treatment of choice for many people. For the non-ABA parent, one must adopt a different stance than the all-business approach appreciated by the ABA parent.

When addressing the non-ABA parent (before they are converted to becoming ABA parents, that is), DO dress formally. A doctor who is going to be discussing their child's condition is expected to conform to a certain etiquette. DO show happy video. DO emphasize long-term goals, but DO aim at small successes at first. DO know non-ABA treatments and discuss them and bend over backwards to do so fairly. DO attempt to provide early success. DO know practical basics that are likely to be troubling parents; be prepared to whip out a toilet training program at a moment's notice. DO use examples from outside the world of autism to explain concepts. DO dispel myths (e.g., that ABA squashes a student's will, or that ABA is only for very low-functioning students).

DON'T hit these parents with too much jargon. Speak in everyday terms. DON'T disparage unproven treatments they might have been trying. DON'T show rough examples too early. DON'T give too much homework too soon. DON'T make requests the parents are not likely to carry out. DON'T emphasize animal models of behavior. DON'T give a "cookbook," explain that individualized programming is the hallmark of ABA.

The New Age

If any individual seems to represent the antithesis of the behavior analyst, it would be the person we would describe as New Age. Practitioners of channeling (the dead speaking through the living), users of healing crystals, tracers of their past lives and visitors with extraterrestrials would hardly seem to have much in common with the scientific behavior analysts. Just as Jesus ate with the tax collectors, however, it is necessary to preach beyond the choir. I therefore have given talks about behavior analysis at New Age conferences, to surprisingly good reception.

To speak to the New Age, there are several important Do's and Don'ts. These can be somewhat "unconventional conventions." Feel free to dress as you feel comfortable. DO use humor. Inspired by Niles, and in view of the negative image many have of the behavior analyst, I have been known to introduce myself as the "Dark

Overlord of Behavior Analysis." At such conferences, you are not judged solely by your data, but by the manner of your presentation and your personal qualities as well. A little humor makes you more human and begins to attack the myth.

On a similar topic, DO show happy video of your work. Behavior analysis improves the lives of those it touches. Feel free to show this. I've had people at the New Age conferences comment on all the wonderful energy between the student and I. Funny, I thought I was just delivering enthusiastic verbal reinforcers. On a related topic, DO emphasize the reinforcing value of watching students progress on your own behavior.

DO emphasize the fact that we are teaching students skills that will give them the ability to make choices in the future. One of the talks that had the greatest impact on my interactions with those outside the ABA field was given by Jon Bailey in 1991, entitled <u>Promoting freedom and dignity: A new agenda for behavior analysis</u>. He spoke of how the behavior analyst is frequently not the most popular person on the treatment team, while the social worker frequently sounds the most noble. "Watch the social workers," Jon advised. Speak as they do. They speak of giving people choices, of building autonomy. Can someone who lacks skills, in reality, have a choice or any autonomy at all? If I don't know how to toilet independently, how can I choose whether or not to do it? How better to give someone a choice than to actually teach them new skills so that they *really* have the choice? DO describe self-management research and emphasize building autonomy and reaching potential.

DO show emotion when you are speaking. At the last New Age conference at which I spoke, I told the story of David and the Seder where his family watched him eat and heard him speak for the first time at this most important family ritual. I'll admit that while I was speaking, I got a little choked up thinking about the phone messages and notes I got from David's mother and the images and emotions they described and had to stop speaking for a few seconds as I collected a new overhead. When I looked up, several people in the audience were crying and holding each other. Their image of the behavior analyst as the evil doctor from <u>A Clockwork Orange</u> was forever blown. DO read articles by Kenneth McCorquodale, Willard Day, and Skinner from <u>The Humanist</u> in the early 1970's. They address the issue of ABA as the granter of autonomy.

DON'T disparage what might seem to be far-out ideas. At the last conference, a woman came up to me to mention that she wanted help with obsessive-compulsive behavior. She had been told by a psychic that she always checked the stove because in a prior life she had been burned alive and in this life it was her karma to seek effective therapy. Who was I to argue? It committed her to the behavior therapy process.

DON'T get too abstract. Keep it to individual progress and use everyday language and examples. DON'T present ABA as the only way in the world, demonstrate how it fits into a wider world view and the rest will follow.

Speaking to Other Cultures

My own experience in discussing ABA with people outside the United States almost exclusively centers around the issues of autism and ABA. What I have found, by and large, is that the important distinction between ABA and non-ABA parents still holds, with almost the same characteristics as are seen in U.S. parents.

When one is speaking about ABA to other cultures, DO become familiar with the unique pressures facing these parents. I have found myself speaking about the power of ABA to parents who desperately want it, but find almost nothing in the way of ABA services in their country other than what they themselves have created by hiring consultants from the U.S. to come over and train themselves and their workers. One must be sensitive to the frustration such a situation can cause and be prepared to discuss how one can do the best one can with what is available. DO emphasize all the good that can be done simply by restructuring the home and family routine, and by training parents and other family members to work directly with the children.

A second concern borders on the humorous. DO learn the expressions of the particular culture. The first training I was providing in Northern Ireland was going rather well, I thought. Everyone was excited and really seemed to be grasping the concepts. I was fielding questions from parents about their children's behavior, and all seemed to be going swimmingly. Even the jokes were working. One mother then described her son's behavior, and finished her description by saying "At the end of the day, he's not talking." What I did *not* know is that "at the end of the day" is an expression in Northern Ireland that means "the bottom line" or "to sum up". Not armed with this crucial information, I said something brilliant to the effect of, "Well, does he talk in the morning?" One hundred people stared at me, thinking aloud "We brought this guy over here for what?" A similar situation was created when a parent asked about "learning disabilities," which in the U.S. refer to specific skills, but in Northern Ireland referred to mental retardation.

An obvious third DO, is to learn the common roles and expectations of family members in the culture. You kill chances of success if you introduce a completely foreign description of child-rearing practices in the very beginning. Obviously, DON'T disparage their cultural practices. There may be discrepancies between your viewpoint and theirs on certain issues, aversives for example. DON'T have a knee-jerk reaction, but rather be prepared to discuss the pro's and con's even-handedly.

Martial Artists

I would like to discuss how one might apply this thinking to people in particular sub-fields, people with special interests. ABA can be applied in areas where it has not traditionally reached, provided we speak and act properly. Over the past few years, I have been studying and writing on topics in the martial arts. Far from being unrelated to the field, I found that there was tremendous overlap between the ideas of many martial arts and applied behavior analysis.

There are many different types of martial arts. They each have an underlying philosophy from which the techniques of various arts stem. Tai Chi, for example, emphasizes the internal chi energy. The slow, graceful movements that we associate with Tai Chi are a logical outgrowth of that underlying belief system. Judo emphasizes "bending without breaking." The redirection of force that is characteristic of judo stems from this philosophy. The "martial art" of behavior analysis holds a deterministic philosophy, and its techniques logically flow from this assumption.

About two years ago, I published a workbook of task analyses of the techniques of an art that I study known as Dragon Kenpo. The workbook was very well-received and led to requests for articles on ABA from <u>Black Belt</u> magazine and <u>Karate International</u>, where I was eventually offered a role as a regular writer. In this column, I speak about the principles of ABA and how they can be applied to effectively teach technique, as well as help students and instructors to understand behavior in a more general sense.

Do's and don'ts: DO dress formally. Unless you are giving an exhibition, you are expected to show respect for others by dressing in a formal manner when speaking. DO use your full academic title and degree. There is a respect for learning in the traditional arts, and thus this is the only arena of my life where I generally use the title, "Professor." DO cite your "pedigree." There is an inherent respect for tradition and one's teachers. "I am Newman, student of Poulson, student of Baer..." DO wax philosophical and cite examples from the natural world. Martial artists tend to think in general philosophical terms, and relate well to concepts that have wide-reaching implications. DO emphasize the effectiveness of behavior analytic teaching. Bruce Lee, possibly the most influential martial artist of this century, advised his students to study all disciplines, to keep that which was useful, and to discard the rest. In addition to waxing philosophical, there is a respect for the pragmatic.

<u>Physical Trainers</u>

A few years ago, I published an article in <u>American Fitness</u> magazine, the magazine of the Aerobics and Fitness Association of America. The article dealt with personal training for a person with autism. That article led to an involvement in the physical training, and a continuing education course for both the Aerobics and Training Association of America and the American Council on Exercise. Speaking to physical trainers about ABA is relatively straight-forward.

DO emphasize results. ABA is a very powerful science for teaching new skills and maintaining behavior. This is what physical trainers are seeking. DO emphasize technique, contingency contracts for example, with an emphasis on safety. Very generally speaking, we are not emphasizing the greater implications, theories or history of ABA, but rather the development of particular techniques.

DON'T discuss animal models of behavior. This is a skill-impartation model, where the students generally are concerned more about the development of practical skills than the greater implications of the system.

Ethical Culture

As I began this discussion by speaking of my experiences with the Ethical Culture Society, it seems fitting to end with them. DO emphasize naturalism, these are people who pride themselves on avoiding all supernaturalism and staying grounded in empirical phenomena. As with the New Age, emphasizing the fostering of individual choice and autonomy is paramount. As Ethical Culture individuals are concerned with societal progress, speaking of Walden Two and general notions of societal progress is excellent fodder for discussion. DO dispel myths about Skinner and ABA. DO emphasize the earlier philosophical traditions, as well as more current behavior analytic research into verbal and cognitive phenomenon. I always keep a copy of The Analysis of Verbal Behavior for explanation purposes, so that people can see beyond their simplistic views of ABA. DON'T get bogged down in useless discussions regarding determinism and free will. Stick to the empirical phenomena. DON'T get bogged down in discussions of manipulation, emphasize reciprocal control.

Summation

ABA has suffered from bad public relations over the years. The movies and books have made for interesting science fiction, but little science fact. Nonetheless, the image of the behavior analyst is as outlined at the beginning of this chapter. With proper considerations, however, the benefits of ABA can become apparent. The goal of any such interaction is showing people what ABA has to offer, and not winning an argument or proving a point. The power of ABA can stand on its own, once people can be convinced to give it a chance. If you plan your talk by considering the goals and background of each group, they will give ABA that chance.

Chapter Twenty: Dan has an in-home ABA Program, Gets Mainstreamed

The "holy grail" of ABA work with children with autism is "recovery," the loss of all symptoms and signs of autism. First demonstrated in a systematic fashion in the famous Lovaas (1987) "Young Autism Project" study, where roughly one half of a sample of children with autism lost all vestiges of their prior diagnoses and became indistinguishable from any typically developing person, "recovery" has become the goal of parents and ABA programs serving people with autism. The unfortunate fact is that recovery has not been systematically demonstrated in students who are older than preschool age. While enormous, life-altering gains can be achieved (see some of the case studies described previously), as students become older, the possibility of full recovery becomes more and more of remote possibility.

Serious efforts have therefore been directed towards preschool students, where the chances for recovery are maximized. While many states do offer early intervention (EI) services, they are often wholly inadequate both in terms of time and the training and technique of the workers. This has led to a deplorable state wherein parents must sometimes sacrifice nearly everything from their own private resources to provide the services their children need. This is the field of "in-home" programming, a multi-million dollar industry that operates largely off the books. Parents mortgage their homes to pay for therapy, and there is little chance for reimbursement.

The birth of the field of in-home programming has been a mixed blessing. On the one hand, many more students than ever before are getting intensive intervention when it can do the most good. On the other hand, much of this programming is of extremely dubious quality. Because behavior analysis is not a legally controlled discipline in most states, anyone can claim to be a behavior therapist, behavior analyst, or even a "Lovaas therapist" without any fear of censure. Many "programmers" have woefully inadequate training, often only having served as assistants for a short time in a school or other in-home program. Because of the lack of a state-recognized behavior analyst credential, there is little other than word-of-mouth or testimonials to prove one's skill and background.

There are signs that this situation is improving. Florida paved the way by first certifying behavior analysts, and a few other states have followed suit. There is an effort on the national level by the international Association for Behavior Analysis (ABA) to certify behavior analysts, and I think I can safely say we all hope that soon parents will have something other than word-of-mouth to use as a measuring stick of therapist quality and background. For the time being, though, it is a "let the buyer beware" market. In my role as editor of <u>The Behavioral Programmer</u>, I oversaw a survey of the state of in-home programming. The most common fee paid for programming was nearly $50 an hour, and the educational level of this person rarely exceeded the bachelor's level (although many were Masters *students* or had recently completed their Masters). A collection of parents had very uncomplimentary things to say about one such individual, who was charging $75 an hour, and a considerable sum for her questionably trained assistants. "After all this time, he still stims every second you're not prompting him to keep his hands down" was one parent's lament at the lack of behavioral skill demonstrated, despite a yearly bill that of about $88,000! How does such a situation exist? It is a simple matter of supply and demand. There are not enough trained behavior analysts in some sections of the country to satisfy the need. Even given legislation to oversee the field, there unfortunately will probably always be dubiously trained "mavericks" who will offer their services to those who cannot afford, or find, a certified individual.

I was contacted in 1995 to create and oversee an in-home program for Dan, a young boy diagnosed with autism. I came to Dan's home to meet him. He was a slightly built, good looking boy. His family were Orthodox Jews, and Dan wore clothing appropriate to that religion. He had a new-born baby brother, and a family who obviously loved him very much. Both his parents were very involved in his development, and spent a great deal of time with him, trying to teach him the skills that would allow him to function in mainstream settings. Dan was luckily enrolled in a preschool with a talented teacher who was knowledgeable about ABA.

The first day I sat down to work with Dan, I could see that he had great potential. Although he pulled out some of my hair and scratched a gash into my face, he quickly responded to an extinction and redirection intervention. While he engaged in a great deal of perseverative behavior, he had verbal imitation skills, a good prognostic sign. Dan's typical vocalizations, however, revolved around echolated statements of rules (e.g., "and you can't turn on the fan, you only wear a shabbos shirt on shabbos"). Dan took great pleasure in his religion, and seemed to really enjoy the rituals.

We began working on very simple skills. Dan would learn to imitate gestures and then appropriate play with toys. In the opening round, we also worked on his being able to establish and maintain eye contact, to "match," to take turns in a game play context, to perform specified actions, to answer questions appropriately, to use "yes" and "no" appropriately, and to make and return social greetings.

As Dan mastered skills, programming became more sophisticated. As Dan mastered action commands, for example, we began to work on pronouns. We would ask Dan "clap your hands." As Dan was clapping, we would ask "what are you doing?" He had to learn to say "I am clapping my hands." This particular drill led to an amusing incident where a wonderful therapist named Naama discovered Dan urinating in his brother's room. In shock, she asked "What are you doing?" Dan thought for a moment and said something to the effect of "I am going on my brother's carpet." By all accounts, he then waited for his reinforcer, as he had performed the drill correctly.

Programming continued to get more sophisticated over the course of time. Body part identification drills turned into drills of "my" and "your". Object identification became object function and letter and number identification. Letter identification became sight words and then phonics. One to one correspondence and graphomotor drills became written math examples and writing words and sentences. Memory drills where Dan had to remember objects that had been removed from the table while his eyes were closed became conversation about prior events. Educational achievement tests as well as standardized intelligence measures were employed to try to assess skill development as well as lagging areas. A lag in spatial-perceptual skills demonstrated by these tests was addressed via the creation of specialized programs (e.g., block design, jigsaw puzzles). Early academic programs and more advanced play and social initiations became the bulk of our time.

Far beyond the use of standardized tests, social validation measures were used. Dan went to the park to play with other children, and mixed with other children at temple. While following instructions in the group proved difficult at first, this was a skill that improved. When Dan aged out of preschool, it was time to pick a school. We all agreed to try to mainstream Dan at a local yeshiva.

Here was where the frustrations of dealing with the school systems can really get to you. Dan had lost most of the "autistic" behavior, and truly did not qualify for the diagnosis any longer. He would have been more properly considered as having an attention deficit and a mild language delay. This was a good thing, as he could not be included in the mainstream class with the diagnosis of autism. He was not ready to function independently in school, however, and would require a "transitional aide." He could not have the aide, however, unless he had a diagnosis of autism. It was the old Catch 22: no mainstream class with the diagnosis, but none of the necessary support unless you had the diagnosis. Fortunately, this situation was able to be resolved after discussion with the very understanding faculty who truly wished to help Dan. The transitional aide was put into place in the kindergarten.

Unfortunately, things were not always smooth sailing. There was limited time to train the aides, and no one on staff at the yeshiva to provide the necessary instruction for the aides. The teacher made some classic mistakes as she tried to implement behavior treatment plans. When told to reinforce appropriate behavior, for example, she would first wait for Dan to behave inappropriately, and then reinforce "calming down." This is a classic mistake, forgetting to reinforce appropriate behavior and instead of being proactive, being reactive and reinforcing the "act out then calm down" unit. Two aides had to be replaced during the year, also undermining stability and consistency. Kindergarten did not allow for the fading out of the transitional aide as we had hoped and planned. Dan still could get lost in the group and not attend to teacher instruction. He was better in the 1-to-1 situation than in the group, but we were hesitant to provide a great deal of 1-to-1 instruction so as to not make him dependent upon it.

First grade brought a more structured teacher, and a steadier aide. Various medications were attempted to address lagging behavior (e.g., to try to increase attentiveness in the group). These had some temporary effects, but nothing that truly "worked miracles" was found. The aide was faded during this time, with less and less of the day requiring an aide. As of the writing of this work, Dan is still pressing along in the mainstream class. He will either make it in this class and continue to keep up with his peers, or he might have to go into a class for those with mild language delays. Whichever happens, he is now ready for a rich and normal life.

Dan did not have the 40 hours a week of intensive intervention that is often cited as the requirement for maximum improvement. This begs the question of "how much" ABA is really necessary. This rather straight-forward question is actually meaningless. How many hours are necessary? There is a simple answer:

ALL OF THEM.

ABA is a 24 hour a day philosophy and set of techniques. A student can have wonderful 1-to-1 programming for a large number of hours a week, and when he is not in program no one works with him or bothers to carry through on a treatment plan if he is behaving inappropriately. This person will not make the same progress as a student who has fewer hours of 1-to-1 programming, but has the rest of his time structured to carry through on the programming and behavior management he does have. There are limits to this logic, of course. Six hours a week of even the highest quality programming is not likely to lead to recovery. On the other hand, quantity is no measure of quality. I have personally witnessed 56 hour a week home programs where students were still not toilet-trained after two

118

years. I've seen intensive programs where students were unable to interact with other students, but knew that the opposite of "alive" is "dead." Let's remember a crucial fact of life: it's more important that you can do the basics than be brilliant. It's probably better to have a GED and be able to interact with others than to have the equivalent of a college degree but be dependent on everyone around you for even basic needs. In this case, it's better to be cool than to be a genius.

As a final note on this issue of ABA and recovery, criticisms of the Lovaas study bear mentioning. There are those who dispute the Lovaas data, citing weaknesses in his experimental design. The students with autism, for example, were supposedly not placed into groups randomly but rather on the basis of whether or not there was an available individual to oversee services. While this is something of a flaw from a technical standpoint, let's not lose the forest for the trees. Show me another study that demonstrated recovery in nearly 50% of the participants and I'll be happy to discuss such "flaws" with you all day.

This ABA stuff works.

References

Aggeler, G. (1979). <u>Anthony Burgess: The artist as novelist</u>. University, Alabama: University of Alabama Press.

Bailey, J. S. (1991). Promoting freedom and dignity: A new agenda for behavior analysis. Paper presented at the 1991 convention of the Association for Behavior Analysis.

Cooper, J. O., Heron, T. L., & Heward, W. L. (1987). <u>Applied behavior analysis</u>. Toronto: Merrill Publishing.

Lovaas, O. I. (1987). Behavioral treatment and normal educational and intellectual functioning of young autistic children. <u>Journal of consulting and clinical psychology</u>, <u>55</u>, 3-9.

Newman, B. (1992). <u>The reluctant alliance: Behaviorism and humanism</u>. Buffalo: Prometheus Books.

Newman, B., Buffington, D. M., & Hemmes, N. S. (1996). External and self-reinforcement used to increase the appropriate conversation of autistic teenagers. <u>Education and Training in Mental Retardation and Developmental Disabilities</u>, <u>31</u>, 304-309.

Newman, B., Buffington, D.M., Hemmes, N.S., & Rosen, D. (1997). Answering objections to self-management and related concepts. <u>Behavior and Social Issues</u>, <u>6</u>(2), 85-95.

Newman, B., Buffington, D.M., O'Grady, M.A., McDonald, M.E., Poulson, C.L., & Hemmes, N.S. (1995). Self-management of schedule-following in three teenagers with autism. <u>Behavioral Disabilities</u>, <u>20</u>(3), 195-201.

Newman, B., Ryan C. S., Tuntigian, L., Reinecke, D.R. (1997). Self-management of a DRO procedure by students with autism. <u>Behavioral Interventions</u>, <u>12</u>(3), 149-156.

Newman, B. (1996). <u>No virtue in accident: Behavior analysis and utopian literature</u>. New York: Dove and Orca.

Petix, E. (1987). Linguistics, mechanics, and metaphysics: A Clockwork Orange. In H. Bloom (Ed.) <u>Modern critical views: Anthony Burgess</u> (pp. 85-96). New York: Chelsea House.

Reinecke, D. R., Newman, B. & Meinberg, D. L. (in press). Self-management of sharing in three preschoolers with autism. <u>Education and Training in Mental Retardation and Developmental Disabilities</u>.

Sidman, M. (1989). <u>Coercion and its fallout</u>. Boston: Authors Cooperative.

Skinner, B. F. (1971). Humanistic behaviorism. <u>The Humanist</u>, <u>31</u>(3), 35.

Wine, S. T. (1985). <u>Humanistic Judaism</u>. Farmington Hills, Michigan: Society for Humanistic Judaism.

Epilogue: A Tribute to B. F. Skinner

I worked on this book with a working title of "Case Studies of ABA with People with Autism" (Keep It Simple, Sir). I vaguely knew it would need a better hook, but couldn't think of anything catchy and didn't want to call it "The Lone Locust of the Apocalypse". As I look back on this work and the past ten years, "When everybody cares" just presents itself. The title is actually taken from the closing comments made by Richard Foxx at the end of the famous "Harry" film, where he discusses the fact that there is no mystery as to why behavior analytic procedures are effective or under what conditions treatment gains are maintained. He rightfully notes that it occurs when "everyone cares and commits to the program."

Despite my immense respect for Dr. Foxx and my tendency to rip off his work (a tendency which has only increased over the years), the real inspiration for this work was B. F. Skinner. As this is a book of stories, it seems only fitting to finish with a story about Dr. Skinner.

I began my career too late to get to know B. F. Skinner. By the time I became active in the field of Applied Behavior Analysis, Skinner was in his final years and seldom attending the conferences. In 1989, though, I signed a contract with Prometheus Books to publish my first book, <u>The Reluctant Alliance: Behaviorism and Humanism</u>. Nervous that I had possibly written something stupid and not wanting to look like an idiot, I sent the manuscript to Dr. Skinner to look over.

I really didn't expect an answer. I knew Dr. Skinner had to be very busy, and had no reason to believe that he would take many hours out of his schedule to read a book-length manuscript from a graduate student he had presumably never heard of. I was therefore very gratified (and a little stunned) when I received a letter back from Dr. Skinner a few months later.

Dr. Skinner actually apologized for the fact that it took him a little while to get back to me. He explained that he was quite ill, in fact he was dying, and that his vision was no longer very acute. He had, however, muddled through the manuscript with some help and offered commentary and encouragement. That's a class act, to take time out from dying to comment on a book-length manuscript from a student one has never heard of. That's also the commitment he felt to the field of Applied Behavior Analysis.

The popular stereotype of Dr. Skinner is that he was a cold man, a distant intellectual. Myths about the man abound. I heard a story as an undergraduate that he had driven his daughter insane by raising her in a box and that she had subsequently committed suicide. The professor who told me that story should have accompanied me to my first ABA convention where I was introduced to Skinner's daughter (who is also a highly accomplished behavior analyst). For an insane corpse, she looked great (or for a living sane person, for that matter). Another story describes Skinner having lunch. Someone came over to say "hello." Skinner looked up from his food, didn't see an idea, and wordlessly went back to eating. Presumably, all he cared about were ideas - not people.

Skinner said that he got used to such misrepresentations and even downright slander. I don't. This was a man who cared deeply and behaved in a fashion that we would all do well to emulate. I would like to close this collection with a favorite quote of mine from an article of Skinner's regarding behavior analysts , which, appropriately, appeared in a magazine called <u>The Humanist</u> (1971, p. 35):

"A gentle people, deeply concerned with the problems facing us in the world today, who see a chance to bring the methods of science to bear on these problems."

It has been suggested that behavior analysts might need a new term to refer to their discipline. The popular image of the evil behaviorist is inextricably tied to the term "applied behavior analyst." In a previous work (Newman, 1992), I suggested that behavior analysis has links to the humanist community that are largely unrecognized. Could this new term be "Humanistic behavior analysis?" While seemingly awkward, and even an oxymoron to some, there is a precedent. Rabbi Sherwin Wine talks of "Humanistic Judaism," a sect of Judaism that emphasizes the historical, scholarly, ethical, and literary tradition of Judaism without a reliance on the ritual and supernaturalism. If Judaism can do it, behavior analysis can do no less. B.F. Skinner himself was named The Humanist of the Year by the American Humanist Association in the early 1970's, so why not Humanistic Behavior Analysis?

Study Guide

This is a listing of the major topics which appear in the chapters of this book. Thanks to AMAC Executive Director Frederica Blausten for suggesting this addition.

FOREWORD: Echolalia, applied behavior analysis vs. psychology

CHAPTER 1: Food refusal, premack reinforcement, generalization

CHAPTER 2: Compulsions, social significance

CHAPTER 3: Contingencies, extinction, extinction burst, DRO, intermittent vs. continuous reinforcement

CHAPTER 4: Reinforcer selection, types of reinforcer, deprivation, satiation, contingent and noncontingent reinforcement

CHAPTER 5: How reinforcers change over time

CHAPTER 6: Social appropriateness, generalization

CHAPTER 7: Baseline, functional analysis

CHAPTER 8: Shaping, forward and backward chaining

CHAPTER 9: Behavioral measures

CHAPTER 10: Compliance training, generalization

CHAPTER 11: Time out from positive reinforcement

CHAPTER 12: Motor imitation, program objective

CHAPTER 13: Premack reinforcers, DRO

CHAPTER 14: Language instruction, fading

CHAPTER 15: Plan application

CHAPTER 16: DRL, intermittent reinforcement, negative reinforcement

About the Author

Bobby Newman is a behavior analyst specializing in early interventions for children with autism. He is the Director of Training for the Association in Manhattan for Autistic Children and a Co-Founder of Room to Grow. He was formerly a crime victim counselor in New York State. His first book, The Reluctant Alliance: Behaviorism and Humanism, was published by Prometheus Books in 1992. His second book, No Virtue in Accident: Behavior Analysis and Utopian Literature was published by Dove and Orca in 1996. He was New York State's first Certified Behavior Analyst and is the editor of The Behavioral Programmer, a popular newsletter describing behavioral interventions for people with autism.

Dr. Newman is on the adjunct faculty of Queens College, CUNY, and was formerly on the faculty of the College of Aeronautics. He has published numerous papers describing innovative teaching techniques for students with autism. His manual for the training of workers in the field of developmental disabilities is used by agencies throughout the United States, as well as Israel and Northern Ireland. His writings and research have appeared in The Behavior Analyst, Education and Training in Mental Retardation, Psychological Record, Behavioral Disorders, Analysis of Verbal Behavior, Perceptual and Motor Skills, The Humanistic Psychologist, Journal of Sex Education and Therapy, Behavior and Social Issues, The Journal of Autism and Developmental Disorders, The Humanist, Behavior Analysis Digest, Humanistic Judaism, and elsewhere.

About the Agency

The Association in Manhattan for Autistic Children, Inc. (AMAC) was formed in 1961. Since that time, it has grown into a family of services which provide help to people with autistic-spectrum disorders and their families throughout their life-span. AMAC provides intensive preschool programs, an intensive school-age program, afternoon and weekend respite and recreation services, respite weekends, as well as a popular summer camp for children and adults. Additionally, adults are provided supported work, day training, case management, and residential services. Anxious to help as many people in the community as possible, AMAC offers innovative training programs for parents and families, both at the AMAC sites and at local community centers. AMAC also provides training to colleges and medical schools who seek to provide their students with quality, state of the art information. AMAC serves over 350 families at present. A cutting edge research facility, AMAC has also been the subject of several documentaries and published articles regarding demonstrably effective, behaviorally based instruction for people with autistic-spectrum disorders.

For further information about AMAC and its family of services, please contact Frederica Blausten, Executive Director, at:

AMAC
25 West 17th Street
New York, NY 10011
212-645-5005

See us on the web at WWW.AMAC.ORG

3532820

Made in the USA